The Next Conservatism

Other titles of interest from St. Augustine's Press

The Next Conservatism

Paul M. Weyrich & William S. Lind

ST. AUGUSTINE'S PRESS
South Bend, Indiana
2009

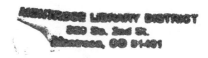

Manufactured in the United States of America.

1 2 3 4 5 6   14 13 12 11 10 09

Library of Congress Cataloging in Publication Data
Weyrich, Paul M.
The next conservatism /
Paul M. Weyrich and William S. Lind.
p. cm.
Includes index.
ISBN-13: 978-1-58731-561-9 (hardbound: alk. paper)
ISBN-10: 1-58731-561-0 (hardbound: alk. paper)
1. Conservatism – United States. 2. United States – Politics
and government – 2001– I. Lind, William S. II. Title.
JC573.2.U6W47 2009
320.520973 – dc22   2009000078

∞ *The paper used in this publication meets the minimum requirements
of the American National Standard for Information Sciences –
Permanence of Paper for Printed Materials, ANSI Z39.48-1984.*

ST. AUGUSTINE'S PRESS
www.staugustine.net

Contents

Paul M. Weyrich, R.I.P.

Paul Weyrich died on December 18, 2008, after this book was written but before its publication. It stands as his last political testament.

The book reflects a series of fifty essays on the next conservatism Paul and I wrote over the past several years. More, it embodies a discussion about politics and a great deal more than politics that we carried on for more than three decades.

I first met Paul Weyrich in 1974 when we were both U.S. Senate staffers. A mutual friend insisted we get together, not because of our shared conservative politics but because of our mutual love of electric streetcars. From the time we were boys, we both realized the trolley cars were going away and we both lamented the fact. Paul's political baptism came when, in his late teens, he attempted to save the famous North Shore Line interurban that served his hometown of Racine, Wisconsin. That effort failed, but one of the joys of Paul's later years was the return of streetcars to cities across America. Not for the last time, Paul had been right too soon.

I cannot attempt to count the hours we spent together over the years, discussing everything from Russell Kirk's books to new designs for the interiors of Amtrak's parlor cars (we came up with a pretty good one). His passing leaves an unfillable void not only in the conservative movement but in my life as well.

In the end, while we did not agree on every issue, our minds worked in parallel to a remarkable degree. I last spoke with Paul on Monday evening of the week of his death. He called me, laughing, to say, "Well, it's finally happened. We bought each other the same book for Christmas."

The Next Conservatism may well have occupied Paul Weyrich's final conscious thoughts. The column he wrote the day he died was titled, "The Next Conservatism: A Serious Agenda for the Future." It concludes,

> It is the worst of times because conservatives appear lost and without a serious agenda or a means of explaining such an agenda to the public. It is the best of times because Free Congress Foundation [which Paul led] has a serious agenda called the Next Conservatism which should ignite a meaningful debate about the future.

Those were his last written words.

Rest in peace, old friend. I have no doubt you are now operating on the North Shore Line, a big grin on your face, running through fields of asphodel.

William S. Lind
December 31, 2008

Introduction

What can someone possibly mean by the "next conservatism"? Isn't conservatism the rejection of change? How can conservatism itself change and remain conservatism?

The imperfect world in which we live is always in flux. If conservatism is to fulfill its duty to conserve what Russell Kirk, borrowing from T.S. Eliot, called "the permanent things," it must do so in the world as we find it. In the first decade of the 21st century, that world faces conservatives, and everyone else, with a new set of issues and challenges.

The conservative agenda that has carried over from the 20th century was itself different from conservatism in the 19th century or the 18th century. Ronald Reagan probably would not have been elected President in 1980 on a platform of upholding the legitimacy of the House of Stuart over that of the House of Hanover.

Reagan's victory was the culmination of a great deal of intellectual work on the part of American conservatives, work that began in the 1950s with Russell Kirk's publication of *The Conservative Mind* and William F. Buckley's founding of *National Review*. Bit by bit, working patiently in what everyone told them was a hopeless cause, American conservatives of the 1950s and 1960s put together a new, relevant conservative agenda. It addressed such post-World War II challenges as the Cold War and the threat of global Communism, the spreading social pathologies generated by the welfare state and the dangers posed by Leviathan, the ever-more-powerful federal government. That agenda, represented by Senator Barry Goldwater, did the impossible and captured the Republican nomination in 1964. Further strengthened intellectually by more ideas, including supply-side economics and a focus on preserving the traditional family, it rose from Goldwater's defeat to elect Ronald Reagan in 1980. Expanded yet again with concepts such as welfare reform and Congressman Newt Gingrich's "Contract with America," it gave the Republican Party control of both Houses of Congress in 1994, for the first time in almost half a century. As Richard Weaver said, "ideas have consequences."

So, however, does a dearth of ideas. Liberalism was defeated in the 1980s and 1990s because it dawdled with an agenda largely devised in the 1930s, the core of which was the politics of envy. The collapse of Newt Gingrich's revolution in the confrontation with President Bill Clinton over the federal government shut-down brought on a similar conservative intellectual lassitude. (The Republicans' response should have been to fire all federal government workers Clinton had designated as "non-essential," thereby achieving at a stroke the reduction in the size of the federal government conservatives had labored for over decades.) As the end of the Cold War, the collapse of Communism and the world-wide triumph of free-market economics realized much that conservatives had worked for from the 1950s onward, the conservative agenda lay stagnant and inert. Conservatism failed to adapt to its own success.

The vacuum was filled, as vacuums will be, but with rubbish. It was filled, first, by a complacent, idea-free, Republican "I've got mine" smugness; with the dragon

2

Fafnir in *Das Rheingold*, Republican office-holders grumbled, "Leave me be; I lie in possession."

The second load of fill-dirt was worse. Conservatism had become so weak in ideas that during the presidency of George W. Bush, the word "conservative" was applied with scant objection to policies that were starkly anti-conservative. Americans witnessed "conservative" Wilsonianism, if not Jacobinism, in foreign policy and an unnecessary foreign war; record "conservative" trade and federal budget deficits; major "conservative" expansions of the power of the federal government at the expense of traditional liberties (never was a law so nakedly named in Newspeak as the "Patriot Act"); and nonchalant "conservative" de-industrialization of America and dispossession of the middle class in the name of Ricardian free trade and Benthamite utilitarianism. No wonder the American people, and especially the conservative grass roots, are confused and disillusioned by conservatism if these are its actions when in power. Were Russell Kirk still with us, what would he now call himself?

The purpose of the next conservatism, and this book, is to renew the work Kirk, Buckley and others did so well in the 1950s and '60s by looking at the challenges of the 21st century through the lens of "the permanent things." Its goal is a new conservative agenda, and a new conservative movement – more, a new kind of conservative movement, for the new century demands more from conservatives than politics.

Of course, essential aspects of the old conservative agenda carry over. The next conservatism still opposes abortion and supports traditional marriage. It seeks further cuts in marginal income tax rates, though it insists on spending cuts as well, and a balanced federal budget. It wants a strong national defense. It demands effective control of our borders, recognizing illegal immigration as the most dangerous single threat to our national security. It seeks to make English our official language, the only language in which government business may be conducted.

All these goals remain important. But they are not sufficient. The next conservative agenda must plow new ground, not because conservatives love innovation – rightly, we regard unnecessary innovation with suspicion – but because the world confronts our country and those who love it with new challenges. The time we must redeem is our own time, not yesterday – though, as we will argue, yesterday has much to offer us if we are willing to remember it.

What are these new challenges? They begin with the fate of the state. Leviathan remains as great a danger as ever, perhaps more so as new technologies permit the state to track and intrude on a scale old-fashioned tyrants could only envy. What indignities will we have to undergo to get on an airplane after the first terrorist employs an explosive suppository?

But to the danger of the state, the 21st century joins something new, the danger to the state. Across the globe, states are in decline. As states wither away in a distinctly non-Marxist fashion, stateless chaos spreads. Conservatism's first virtue is order, and the decline of the state threatens order more profoundly than has anything since the state began its rise in the late 15th century. How ought the next conservatism confront simultaneously the danger of the state and the danger to the state? By restoring the republic, a topic to which this volume will devote considerable thought.

As liberalism has waned, intellectually and politically, its place has been taken by a more potent ideology. Americans' most fundamental freedoms, including freedom

4

of speech and freedom of association, are under threat from the ideology most commonly known as "multiculturalism" or "Political Correctness." But what really is "PC?" A tour through a bit of esoteric intellectual history reveals its secret: it is cultural Marxism, Marxism translated from economic into cultural terms by a think tank established in 1923 in Frankfurt, Germany, the infamous Institute for Social Research. Cultural Marxism's goal from the outset has been nothing less than the destruction of Western culture and the Christian religion, goals toward which it has made frightening progress. The next conservatism must arm Americans against this menace with the weapon it fears most: the revelation of its real nature. If the average citizen finds out that Political Correctness is a variant of Marxism, it will be in trouble.

Just as the next conservatism must confront the threat of ideology, it must also face up to another mortal danger to any republic: a quest for Empire. Driven with equal force by neo-liberals and neo-conservatives, our country has responded to the fall of Communism not as conservatives long expected, by a return to our traditional policy of avoiding foreign entanglements, but by plunging into foreign wars.

Worse, we find ourselves caught up in, and losing, wars of a new type: what military theorists call Fourth Generation wars. While America now spends as much on defense as the rest of the world put together, much of what it buys is for yesterday's wars, wars between the formal armies, navies and air forces of states. Against the non-state forces of the Fourth Generation, most of our high-technology "systems" are proving to be expensive piles of junk. Here, the next conservatism must both reach to the past and look to the future, reviving the foreign policy wisdom of Senator Robert A. Taft and pushing a recalcitrant Pentagon – which now controls the world's largest planned economy – into serious military reform. This book goes into both subjects in necessary detail, proposing nothing less than a new national grand strategy.

While conservatives spent the last several decades winning an impressive series of political victories, the left continued to score triumphs in the war for our culture. Unfortunately, culture is more powerful than politics. The result has been that, while lots of Republicans were elected to office, our country continued to deteriorate. It has declined so far, so fast, that America's future looks increasingly like Brave New World, the "soft totalitarianism" described in the 1930s by Aldous Huxley in a short novel with that title. Brave New World represents nothing less than what C.S. Lewis called the abolition of man.

Any conservatism worthy of the name must be, first and foremost, cultural conservatism. The next conservatism must jump into the culture war with both feet if Judeo-Christian, Western Civilization is to be more than a subject for historians a hundred years from now. Here as elsewhere, there are new challenges to confront:

* America may be a land of plenty, but not plenty of beauty. Modern American art, music, architecture, in high culture and popular culture alike, are too often of an astonishing and alienating ugliness. Why this is so, and how to remedy it, must be a part of the next conservative agenda.

* A new ideology is descending upon the Western world, perhaps the most anti-human of the whole foul brood; environmentalism. In its more extreme variants, it already calls mankind a "cancer" upon the planet. How should the next conservatism confront this monster? Not, we suggest, with yet more materialism and

consumerism, which conservatives have always seen as threats to culture and soul alike, but by reviving an old conservative value: conservation. Conservation, like conservatism itself, is not an ideology but a way of life, one familiar to our forefathers.

* To the hurly-burly of time-pressed modern existence, the next conservatism answers something else rescued from our past, agrarianism. Family farms remain a good place for children to grown up, and the Amish show that they can be economically viable. Small family farms, organic farming, farmers' markets and "crunchy cons," we argue, should have an honored place in the next conservative agenda. Should the next conservative administration seek its Secretary of Agriculture among the Amish instead of from the usual representatives of corporate agri-business?

* Perhaps the most difficult intellectual challenge facing the next conservatism is the effects on our culture of new technologies. Sometimes, these are benign: the internet is a powerful antidote to ideologues who would restrict freedom of thought and expression. But it is not always so. Should conservatives be unconcerned that, after 3,000 years of struggle to replace the image with the word, video screen technologies are rapidly obscuring the word with the image? Genetic engineering threatens frightful catastrophes, from new plagues engineered as weapons of war through offering Brave New World its final, inescapable mechanism of control. The next conservatism, we suggest, must offer means for evaluating new technologies so that we do not allow them indiscriminately to re-shape our lives in ways we may not anticipate and may not want.

To all these and other cultural challenges, the next

conservatism responds not only with dire warnings but with a new tool, one we believe may allow the restoration of our old culture, now in peril. Our term for it is Retroculture. It involves nothing less than re-discovering our past, not in grand sweeps of history but in the ways our forefathers lived their daily lives, as recently as the 1950s – America's last normal decade – and adopting those old ways again. Politics has little to do with Retroculture, but then the next conservatism is not only about politics. The left's cultural revolution, begun in the 1960s, can be met only with cultural restoration, with the recovery of past ways of living. Here, we think, lies the potential not only for a new conservative movement, but a new kind of movement, one that may have more in common with home-schoolers than with Republican politicians.

If culture lies at the heart of the next conservatism, economics is the gut of much of today's conservatism. That is not, we suggest, as it should be. Russell Kirk was by no means the only conservative to believe that life should be about more than getting and spending, lest men be reduced to beasts of the field. The next conservatism seeks to put economics in its place.

At the same time, it faces the economic issues of the 21st century directly. Is Globalism something conservatives should welcome, or even accept? Not unless we wish to see America reduced to a Third World country, we suggest. Conservatives have long recognized the danger of Big Government, but is a "free market" dominated by vast, rootless international corporations truly free? Scale of enterprise will be a major issue in coming years, we think, and the next conservatism should be on the side of the small, the native and the local.

The next conservatism sees economic issues, like political issues, first and foremost as questions of culture. Just as conservatives should oppose destruction of our old culture by anti-human ideologies, so it should defend traditional ways of life from Benthamite efficiency. From Burke to Kirk, efficiency was never a conservative virtue.

The next conservatism, as we offer it here, is a new conservative agenda. But it is more than that. As we suggested at the outset, that agenda should lead to and be embodied in a restored American republic. What, precisely, does that mean? It means a federal government refocused, much against its will, no doubt, on the state's original function: upholding order by providing security of persons and property. That security, we suggest, breaks down into three elements: physical security, which includes national defense; economic security, starting with defending America's economy and jobs from predatory foreigners; and moral security, by which we mean that those who live by our culture's old values and virtues should not find themselves and their families under constant assault. Freedom meets proper limits when it tramples on the rights of others, as it does when it demands the public square become a porn shop.

A restored republic opens the door to the restoration of our culture. But by the nature of a republic's limited government, it cannot itself restore the culture. The left has turned government into an instrument of cultural warfare, but that is an abuse the next conservatism seeks to end.

The only power that can restore our traditional Western, Judeo-Christian culture is the power of example, which is also the only safe form of power. The next conservative movement, as we envision it here, is not only a political movement. It is a gathering of people and families committed to Retroculture, to living life once again in the old ways. By so doing, they can teach our fellow citizens life's most precious lesson: how to live.

If this introduction to the next conservatism, and this book, seem to have a broad sweep, they are intended to. It requires a wide broom indeed to sweep away the cultural and political detritus of the 20th century, history's worst, for the West at least. Nothing less should be our goal, because anything less may slow our nation's and our culture's decline – they are Siamese twins – but will not reverse it. Redeeming the time means restoration, of our republic, our culture, of old ways of living and, ultimately, of our faith. As Russell Kirk wrote, culture comes from the cult.

Carpe diem. And no, that does not mean complain to God.

Chapter One

What Is Conservatism?

Before we begin to define the next conservatism, we need to make clear what we mean by the word "conservatism" itself. The term is now used so broadly that it includes elements and movements that not only are not conservative, they are anti-conservative, to the point of being Jacobin. An attempt to force "democracy" on the rest of the world, by force of arms where necessary, would receive the approbation of Robespierre more easily than that of Edmund Burke.

Here as elsewhere in this book, when we are in need of wisdom we turn to Russell Kirk. Dr. Kirk was the foremost thinker of the post-war American conservative movement. His work deserves more careful attention than it has received, not only from conservatives. He has much to say to all thoughtful men about the problems of our time.

In his book *The Politics of Prudence*, Kirk offers ten conservative principles, to which we subscribe. They offer as good a definition of contemporary American conservatism as we have found. In summary, Dr. Kirk's conservative principles are:

> First, the conservative believes that there exists an enduring moral order . . . human nature is a constant, and moral truths are permanent.

Second, the conservative adheres to custom, convention, and continuity. . . . Order and justice and freedom, [conservatives] believe, are the artificial products of a long social experience, the result of centuries of trial and reflection and sacrifice. . . . Human society is no machine, to be treated mechanically. The continuity, the life-blood, of a society must not be interrupted. Burke's reminder of the necessity for prudent change is in the mind of the conservative. But necessary change, conservatives argue, ought to be gradual and discriminatory, never unfixing old interests at once.

Third, conservatives believe in what may be called the principle of prescription . . . that is, of things established by immemorial usage, . . . There exist rights of which the chief sanction is their antiquity, including rights to property, often. Similarly, our morals are prescriptive in great part.

Fourth, conservatives are guided by their principle of prudence . . . . Any public measure ought to be judged by its probable long-term consequences, not merely by temporary advantage or popularity. . . . The conservative declares that he acts only after sufficient reflection, having weighed the consequences. Sudden and slashing reforms are as perilous as sudden and slashing surgery.

Fifth, conservatives pay attention to the principle of variety. They feel affection for the proliferating intricacy of long-established social institutions and modes of life, as distinguished from the narrowing uniformity and deadening egalitarianism of radical systems. For the preservation of a healthy diversity in any civilization, there must survive orders and classes, differences in material condition, and many sorts of inequality.

Sixth, conservatives are chastened by their principle of imperfectability. . . . Man being imperfect, no perfect social order ever can be created. . . . To seek for utopia is to end in disaster, the conservative says: we are not made for perfect things. All that we reasonably can expect is a tolerably ordered, just, and free society, in which some evils, maladjustments, and suffering will continue to lurk.

Seventh, conservatives are persuaded that freedom and property are closely linked. Separate property from private possession, and Leviathan becomes master of all. . . . The more widespread is the possession of private property, the more stable and productive is a commonwealth. Economic leveling, conservatives maintain, is not economic progress. Getting and spending are not the chief aims of human existence; but a sound economic basis for the person, the family, and the commonwealth is much to be desired.

Eighth, conservatives uphold voluntary community, quite as they oppose involuntary collectivism. . . . In a genuine community, the decisions most directly affecting the lives of citizens are made locally and voluntarily. . . . When these functions pass by default or usurpation to centralized authority, then community is in serious danger. . . .

Ninth, the conservative perceives the need for prudent restraints upon power and upon human passions. . . . Knowing human nature for a mixture of good and evil, the conservative does not put his trust in mere benevolence. Constitutional restrictions, political checks and balances, adequate enforcement of the laws, the old intricate web of restraints upon will and appetite – these the conservative approves as instruments of freedom and order.

Tenth, the thinking conservative understands that permanence and change must be recognized and reconciled in a vigorous society. . . . The Permanence of a society is formed by those enduring interests and convictions that give us stability and continuity; without that Permanence, the fountains of the great deep are broken up, society slipping into anarchy. The Progression in a society is that spirit and that body of talents which urge us on to prudent reform and improvements; without that Progresbsion, a people stagnate. . . . The conservative takes care that nothing in a society should ever be wholly old, and that nothing should ever be wholly new. . . . Just how much change a society requires, and what sort of change, depend upon the circumstances of an age and a nation.[1]

To this definition of conservatism we adhere. You will find it reflected in the remainder of this book.

We append another definition, a definition of cultural conservatism. The authors of this book are cultural conservatives. Our primary goal is the defense and, where it has been lost, the restoration of our country's traditional culture. More than twenty years ago, we offered this definition of cultural conservatism, in some essays and two books with that title:

1 Russell Kirk, *The Politics of Prudence* (Wilmington, Del.: ISI Books, 1993), ch. 2, 17 ff.

14

> Cultural conservatism is the belief that there is a necessary, unbreakable, and causal relationship between traditional Western, Judeo-Christian values, definitions of right and wrong, ways of thinking and ways of living – the parameters of Western culture – and the secular success of Western societies: their prosperity, their liberties, and the opportunities they offer their citizens to lead fulfilling, rewarding lives. If the former are abandoned, the latter will be lost.

To both definitions of conservatism, we add a warning: conservatism is not an ideology. Attempts to turn it into one yield something that is anti-conservative. Rather, conservatism is a way of life.

An ideology says that on the basis of this or that philosophy, certain things must be true: a society is shaped solely by who owns the means of production (economic Marxism), Western culture oppresses everyone except white males (cultural Marxism), Aryans are the master race (Nazism), the earth would be a paradise if man were eliminated ("Deep Green" environmentalism). When reality contradicts these ideological "truths," reality must be suppressed. Ideology forbids writing, speaking, or thinking about the contradictions. If the ideology achieves sufficient power, it criminalizes contradictory thought or expression. It demands people live a lie, and dispatches those who will not to "sensitivity training," the gulag or the concentration camp.

In contrast, conservatism reflects reality, as many generations have observed, oriented and adapted to it. Those orientations and adaptations have come down to us as traditions, customs and precedents. They are embodied not in an abstract philosophical system, but in the ways most people live their everyday lives. A living conservatism continually adapts itself to reality through prudent reforms, which, if successful, become new traditions and habits. It is necessary and proper that this process take time. As Dr. Johnson argued, time is the only valid test of the merits of anything.

Let us turn again to Russell Kirk to conclude this short defining chapter. Lest anyone still imagine conservatism and ideology can be reconciled, here is what the good doctor has to say on the matter, again from *The Politics of Prudence*:

> Nay, madam, all ideologies work mischief. I am fortified by a letter from an influential and seasoned conservative publicist, who applauds my excoriation of young ideologues fancying themselves to be conservatives, and of young conservatives fondly hoping to convert themselves into ideologues. This latter correspondent agrees with me that ideology is founded merely upon "ideas" – that is, upon abstractions, fancies, for the most part unrelated to personal and social reality; while conservative views are founded upon custom, convention, the long experience of the human species. . . .

> The triumph of ideology would be the triumph of what Edmund Burke called "the antagonist world" – the world of disorder; while what the conservative seeks to conserve is the world of order that we have inherited, if in a damaged condition, from our ancestors. The conservative mind and the ideological mind stand at opposite poles. And the contest between those two mentalities may be no less strenuous in the twenty-first century than it has been during the twentieth.

Chapter Two

Restore the Republic!

Having recently endured the sad carnival that is an American presidential election, most conservatives would just as soon forget about politics for a while. But the fact that our elections have become carnivals of buncombe tells us we have work to do. Electing this or that candidate achieves little or nothing. We have to fix the system. How? By restoring the republic.

We still pledge allegiance to "the flag and the republic for which it stands," but today America is a republic in name only. Washington has become the seat of a vastly powerful, endlessly intrusive oligarchic government that responds only to monied interests, not average citizens. We don't agree with former California Governor Jerry Brown about much, but when he said, "Unless you have recently given a politician a check for at least $1,000, you don't count," he was exactly right.

Until recently, it was routine for conservatives to warn about the danger from Leviathan, the all-powerful state. The next conservatism needs to revive that warning, and make it stronger. Because of the so-called "war on terrorism," America may be on the verge of becoming a national security state, also known as a "garrison state." The Constitution and the liberties it protects will go out the window as citizens permit the state to do whatever it wants, so long as it justifies its actions in terms of "national security."

Conservatives accept the fact that the state must defend us from terrorism and other acts of war. That has always been one of the state's duties. But the next conservatism does not want "permanent war for permanent peace," as George Orwell put it in 1984. We are not convinced that the best way to defend America from terrorism is by invading and occupying other countries, places with religions and cultures very different from our own.

Our Founding Fathers warned us that we could either preserve our republic and our domestic liberties or play the game of Great Power, but we could not do both. Playing the Great Power game requires a strong central government that can make decisions with little regard for the thoughts or desires of the average citizen. Such a government will run roughshod over our liberties, because it can. Preserving our liberties requires a weak federal government with limited powers, especially in the Executive, and strong internal checks and balances. Such a government by its nature is poorly structured to try to run the whole world.

The next conservatism prefers liberty at home to empire abroad. It recognizes that if we trade our liberties for security, we will end up with neither. While the next conservatism is firmly for measures that will really improve our security, such as taking control of our borders and ending illegal immigration, it rejects the national security state. Our country has survived many wars without discarding the Constitution, and we can do the same in the "war on terrorism" if conservatives insist on it.

What does rejecting the national security state mean? A few actions include:

* We should never again pass wide-ranging legislation that endangers our liberties in the immediate aftermath

of a terrorist attack, as we did with the mis-named "Patriot Act" after 9/11. It is almost certain that, so long as we are intervening in other countries, we will be attacked by terrorists here at home. Some of these attacks may be much worse than 9/11. When they happen, cool heads should prevail over immediate fears. If we allow ourselves to be carried away by our fears, and by voices that will play on those fears to increase the power of the state, we will lose our freedom.

* We must insist that no one, not even the president in his role as Commander-in-Chief, is above the law. Presidents may not exempt themselves from laws they dislike with "signing statements." They may not order torture or other actions that contradict the law, such as holding American citizens in jail without charges or in disregard of *habeas corpus*. A president who breaks the law and violates the rights of American citizens should be impeached.

* We must be very careful about how we allow government to use advanced new technologies, which permit unprecedented powers of surveillance and intrusion. Here, the state may seek to follow the letter of the law (mostly laws written before such technologies could be imagined) while nonetheless undermining our liberties. The next conservatism would prefer to put legal restraints on new technologies before they subvert our liberties and our privacy rather than try to recover lost ground after the fact.

Far from lessening the need for conservatives to be wary of the power of the state, the threat of terrorism should make the next conservatism more wary. If we end up living in a national security state, where anything is permitted in the name of national security, our republic will finally be lost. We will become not a free people but an administered people, like the Russians under the Soviet Union or the Chinese people today. As in Russia then, the government will say to any and all of us, "We have no laws, we only have instructions."

Earlier generations of conservatives would have seconded these warnings about the national security state. They would have pointed as well to another threat: the ideological state. For the first time in its history, America has become an ideological state, which is the opposite of a free republic. The ideology commonly known as "Political Correctness" or "multiculturalism" now shapes the actions of government in countless ways.

Under the rubric of "hate crimes," it sentences American citizens to additional jail time for political thoughts. As "affirmative action," it "privileges" Feminist women, blacks and homosexuals over normal white males. In some cases, it requires private businesses to give their employees "sensitivity training," which means psychologically conditioning them to obey the state ideology, including its demand that everyone express approval of homosexuality. Employees who refuse lose their jobs.

What should the next conservatism do about this ideological *coup d'etat*? First, reveal this ideology for what it is. What people call "Political Correctness" is really cultural Marxism, Marxism translated from economic into cultural terms. We will explore its history in more detail later in this book. Briefly, it was created by the Institute for Social Research, aka the "Frankfurt School," a Marxist think tank established at Frankfurt, Germany in 1923 that moved to New York City in 1934. These renegade (from Moscow's standpoint) Marxists said that, contrary to Marx, culture is not just part of society's "superstructure" but an independent and very important variable. They concluded that for

20

Communism to be possible in the West, traditional Western culture and the Christian religion first had to be destroyed. Important as ideas were to them, they realized they could not destroy our historic culture through philosophical arguments. They turned instead to a much more powerful weapon, psychological conditioning, in effect crossing Marx with Freud. Want to "normalize" homosexuality? Just psychologically condition the public through television show after television show (key Frankfurt School members spent the war years in Hollywood) where the only normal-seeming white male is a homosexual.

Political Correctness is intellectual Soylent Green. The next conservatism needs to shout from the housetops, "People, here's what this stuff really is. It's not about 'being nice' or 'toleration.' It's Marxism, it's about destroying our culture and our religion, and it's succeeding."

Then, when we have the American people behind us, we need to comb through every law, every government regulation and program, every federal office and department and weed the cultural Marxism out. The goal should not be to replace it with any ideology of our own – as conservatives, we do not have one – but to restore a non-ideological American republic, which is what we had up until the wretched 1960s.

Russell Kirk and other conservatives from the 1950s and '60s would say, "Hear, hear." If these aspects of Leviathan might be new to them, they thoroughly understood the threat the state poses to liberty.

But the next conservatism must also face a different problem: the danger *to* the state. If the 21st century develops the way some thoughtful people believe it will, it will see the decline and, in some places, the disappearance of the state itself.

Some conservatives, or more precisely some libertarians, might respond "Hurray!" We disagree. So long as the state is limited in its power (more limited than our federal government is now, but not more than the Constitution intended it to be), it is a good thing. Before the state arose in the 15th century, life was, as Thomas Hobbes put it, nasty, brutish and short. The state arose to bring order and security of persons and property. As conservatives, we think those are good things.

Perhaps the most perceptive writer about the state is the Israeli historian Martin van Creveld. In his book *The Rise and Decline of the State*, he argues that the state has gone through three historical stages. It arose to bring order, which for several centuries it did. But beginning with the French Revolution and the development of abstract nationalism (conservatives are patriots, but not nationalists), the state tried to become a god, to which citizens owed and should sacrifice everything. That false god died in World War I, at places like Verdun. Then, the state reinvented itself as the *alma mater*, the welfare state that would take good care of all its citizens' needs. That also failed, in the failure of socialism and social welfare programs. The state found it could redistribute wealth but could not create it.

With the failure of the welfare state, the state itself now faces a growing crisis of legitimacy. The bureaucratic state begot the "New Class," made up of the kind of people who run Washington regardless of which party is in power. The New Class has three characteristics: it can't make things work (look at America's public schools), it uses its wealth and power to exempt itself from the consequences of things not working (its kids go to private schools) and it really cares about only one thing: remaining the New Class.

As more and more people around the world, including Americans, come to realize that the state has become a racket run for the benefit of the New Class, they are responding by transferring their primary loyalty away from the state. They are transferring it not only to many different things, but to many different kinds of things: to religions (al Qaeda seeks to replace the state with an Islamic Caliphate), to ideologies, to causes such as environmentalism or animal rights, to races and ethnic groups, to gangs and business enterprises, legal and illegal. Often, people who will not fight for the state will fight for their new loyalty. The environmentalist who buries a saw blade in a tree, hoping to kill a logger, is committing an act of war, not merely a crime.

Just as the next conservatism must address the danger *of* the state, it must also offer some answers to the danger *to* the state. The answer is *not* to give the state more power. That just means giving more power to the New Class, which will exacerbate, not diminish, the state's crisis of legitimacy.

In America, restoring the state's legitimacy can only be accomplished by restoring the republic, the limited federal government, respectful of our liberties, our Founding Fathers intended and our Constitution describes. That in turn requires breaking the New Class and its monopoly on power. As we said at the outset, we have to fix the system, not elect Tweedledum in place of Tweedledumber. Examples of the sorts of political reforms the next conservatism should promote include:

* Term limits. The push for term limits on public office-holders has faded, which is unfortunate. A republic needs ordinary citizens in positions of public trust, people whose real lives are back home with the people they represent, not professional politicians who stay in Washington as lobbyists after they leave office. Along with term limits, we should forbid former legislators (and their wives) from working as lobbyists, where

they "cash in" with the interests they helped while in Congress. And we should limit the length of Congressional sessions, so members of Congress spend most of their time back home, not in Washington.

* We should put a new line on every ballot, "None of the above," and if it wins there should be a new election with new candidates. Voters in Russia have the power to reject all candidates, and they sometimes do it. Why should American voters have to hold their noses and pick the lesser of two weevils? NOTA would put pressure on all parties to offer better candidates.

* We need to establish a more level playing field between incumbents and challengers. Incumbents now hold a tremendous advantage, demonstrated by how few are defeated despite the public's dissatisfaction with Congress. One way to level the playing field would be to allow challengers to spend several times as much money on their campaigns as incumbents.

* We also need to create a level playing field for third parties. Third parties have historically played important roles in advancing new ideas. The Republican and Democratic Parties (which are really one party, the Establishment Party) collude in keeping third parties out of the system. The next conservatism should insist on more options for the voters – can you remember an election where you could vote for someone who really believes what you do? – and fair play for all parties.

* To break the power of the New Class, the next conservatism should work to expand the use of ballot initiatives and referenda. They should be made legal in all states and at the federal level as well. That is how Swiss voters keep their government in check, and it could work here. We also need to find ways to prevent

one member of the New Class, a judge, from overturning the people's will in the form of a referendum outcome just because his Establishment buddies do not like it or it contravenes the demands of cultural Marxism.

* We need some effective checks on money politics. We do not mean laws like McCain-Feingold, which is just an incumbents' protection act. We have to put an end to campaign contributions, which the rest of the world rightly calls bribes. Yes, they sell their votes. How to put a stop to it remains a conundrum. But so long as Jerry Brown remains correct, we will never get our republic back. Republics do not have a "pay to play" political process.

This list of reforms is not exhaustive. As the next conservatism develops, other conservatives will come up with more ideas, possibly better than these. The goals in each case should be, first, to displace the New Class and second, to restore the republic. We cannot accomplish the second without doing the first.

Think Locally, Act Locally

Restoring the republic must start in Washington, but if it is to be real, it cannot end there. In a real republic, life is lived locally, and most issues are dealt with at the local level. For many years, the left has had a slogan, "Think globally, act locally." The next conservatism needs to answer this with a slogan of our own: Think locally, act locally.

"Think globally, act locally" reflects the left's centuries-old belief in "One World." As the Jacobins of the French Revolution desired, everyone in the world is to be forced to abandon their traditions and fit one "Globalist" model, based on some ideology (these days, usually a combination of cultural Marxism and environmentalism). We even see some people who call themselves "conservatives" promoting Globalism. Sorry, but that is not what the word "conservative" has meant.

On the contrary, conservatives have always valued local variety. We prize local cultures, traditions and ways of life, reflecting what has grown up in a specific place over generations. We want Maine to be Maine and the Deep South to remain the Deep South, rather than every place becoming California.

The next conservatism needs to help Americans see the value of what is local and traditional. Much of that is not political, but real conservatism has never just been about politics. It is leftist radicals, not conservatives, who want to politicize everything. The conservative way of life is grounded in local traditions, in preserving and, where necessary, restoring those traditions.

At the same time, politics has a role to play, again within the framework of restoring the republic. The next conservatism needs to revive an important conservative principle that has to some extent been lost, even among conservatives: subsidiarity.

Subsidiarity says that decisions should be made at the lowest practicable level. As much as possible should be decided locally. Only when the local level clearly cannot cope should state governments get involved. Federal involvement should be rare, because it is dangerous. Now decisions made in Washington often run roughshod over local rights, needs, traditions and realities.

The next conservatism should promote one powerful action that would do much to restore subsidiarity. It should put an end to all unfunded mandates, on both the state and federal levels. Today, state governments and the federal government lay more and more requirements on local governments, local schools, local transit systems and the like, but they do not provide any funds to meet those requirements. The things local people know are more important go without funding because the local level has no choice but to give the money to these mandates. They are required by law to do so.

It is easy for state and federal lawmakers to please this or that interest group (from which they get money) by creating new mandates in law. It would not be so easy if they had to pay for those mandates themselves. A rule of "No unfunded mandates" would move many decisions away from state and federal levels and back to the local level, where they belong. It would also reduce the power of government generally, which would help restore the republic.

"Think locally, act locally" goes well beyond putting an end to unfunded mandates. It goes well beyond politics. In the end, it is a call for Americans to become citizens again instead of mere consumers, of government services as well as too much else. By thinking locally and acting locally, we create the positive content of a restored republic. Government at all levels has less to do, because active citizens have taken care of problems before they grew too big to manage. That is how real republics work.

The Political Route

At this point, you may say, "Great. All this sounds like what we need to do. So how do we make it happen?" The answer is, "Through politics."

That is a discouraging answer. It is hard to see how anything good could make it through the political system. Washington is controlled by powerful, monied interests that feed off our nation's decay. They will oppose reform with all their influence, because reform might push them away from the public trough. The interests, and the large number of Senators and Congressmen of both parties they own, care nothing about the country as a whole.

But politics is the only road that leads toward our goal, restoring the republic. We have to take that road. The question is, what vehicle should the next conservatism choose in politics, for restoring the republic and for the rest of our agenda?

We have three choices: the Republican Party, the Democratic Party or a third party, perhaps a new conservative party. The third-party route is tempting, but unlikely to succeed. The Republicans and the Democrats together have so stacked the deck against third parties that it would almost take a miracle for one to win. A restored republic would end the two-party (which are for the most part one party) monopoly, but that comes at the end of the road. Right now, we are at the beginning.

That means the next conservatism's political vehicle is most likely going to be the Republican Party. We have to re-take the Republican Party for real conservatism. We have to do again what we did starting in the 1960s and ending in the nomination and election of Ronald Reagan in 1980.

Some Republicans may say, "You don't need to re-take the Republican Party for conservatism. It's conservative now."

Sorry, but we did not get into town on the last truckload of turnips. The professional politicians who control the Republican Party look on real conservatism (and real conservatives) with contempt.

Through the administration of President George W. Bush, the Republican Party we see in Washington (local and state Party organizations are often much more conservative) was right on some issues. President Bush nominated good judges, and most Republicans in the Senate tried to get them confirmed. They did cut taxes. They went through the motions of giving conservatives a hearing.

But there are too many issues where the Republican

Party, openly or covertly, sold conservatives out. The Bush administration's policy of promoting "democracy" (a code-word for Globalism) around the world by force of arms is Wilsonianism, to which conservatives were always opposed. On federal spending, immigration and trade issues, the Republicans could hardly have been worse. On the culture, they tell conservatives they agree with us, but what they say and do behind closed doors is often another story. Many Washington Republicans look on our opposition to Feminism and "gay rights," to name just two cultural issues, with secret derision. They have accepted the rules laid down by cultural Marxism, at least to the point where they do not have the courage to break them.

Truth be told, most Washington Republicans do not hold any core beliefs, beyond believing in themselves and their right to remain members of the New Class. Their only goals are to have a successful career as a professional politician and leave Washington rich. These courtiers' attitude toward the "little people," those who are not writing them $1,000 checks, is "I'm all right, Jack, I've got mine." As one conservative who has watched Washington from the inside for decades put it, the difference between the Democratic Party and the Republican Party is the difference between Madonna and Donald Trump.

Unless we are prepared to be used and then discarded by Republicans over and over, conservatives need to re-take the Republican Party. How can we do that?

At the presidential level, we first have to get behind a candidate. We did not do that before the 2008 nominating process began, so we had lost before it started. We had no dog in the fight, other than Ron Paul, who realistically did not have a chance of gaining the nomination.

The candidate has to be genuinely one of us. He must believe in his heart in real conservatism, including restoring the republic. He must be willing to fight for our issues and articulate our viewpoint, even when the cultural Marxists call him names. He must promise that when elected he will put our people in positions of power.

If we get that kind of commitment, then we should back this candidate in every precinct caucus, beginning in Iowa. We should build a grass-roots organization for him in every state that has a primary.

If we can nominate this candidate and elect him president, then we can take over the Republican Party from the top down, which is a lot easier and faster than doing it bottom-up. Just as George W. Bush appointed Ed Gillespie and then Ken Mehlman, two very able political technicians, as Republican Party Chairmen, our president must appoint the best political technician in the country, someone who knows what to do to re-take the Party for conservatism. Then, we do that state-by-state and eventually precinct-by precinct.

Once we have succeeded in re-taking the Republican Party for real conservatism, we cannot stop. The usual Washington Establishment will try to recapture it from us, telling us what we want to hear while doing the opposite. The way to prevent this is to have an automatic mechanism to force a primary race for any Republican office-holders who abandon our agenda. We have to make it absolutely certain that any Republican who sells us out pays a price.

What about the Democratic Party?

So long as the Democratic Party remains captive to the cultural Marxists, it can have little appeal to conservatives, at least on the national level (there are some very good individual Democratic office-holders). However, because the next conservatism seeks to restore the republic, it should want a Democratic Party that offers a viable alternative to the Republican Party. No party can remain in power for long without becoming at least somewhat corrupt and also losing touch with its grass roots base and their agenda.

Here is our prescription for reviving the Democratic Party and making it a contender among conservatives. We offer these suggestions as "political doctors," suggesting what we think would work for our "patient," not necessarily our personal views on issues.

First, if the Democratic Party wants to be able once again to appeal to a majority of Americans, not just a collection of special interest groups, it needs to dump cultural Marxism. Cultural Marxism condemns as evil whites, Christians, men and non-Feminist women. They represent a majority of American voters. So long as these people know the Democratic Party sees them as "class enemies," they will not support it. Even if bad times get the Democrats in once, they will soon be out again. Cultural Marxism damns the Democratic Party to long-term minority status.

Then, the Democrats need a new platform, one that amounts to more than whining about Republicans. We would recommend the following planks:

* A realistic foreign policy based on interests and prudence, which looks to the likely long-term effects of actions, not just intentions. With Republicans adopting Wilsonianism and fighting "wars of choice," the Democrats have an opportunity to appeal to a majority of voters by opposing adventurism in foreign affairs.
* Military reform, which looks not just at how much we spend on defense but what the money actually buys and whether it is relevant to future wars.
* A policy of long-term financial soundness for the fed-

31

eral government. The programs Democrats favor, such as Social Security and Medicare, depend on this. Republicans' imprudence on government spending opens a door for the Democrats here.

* A pro-growth economic policy, but one that focuses on jobs rather than Wall Street's profits. The quality of jobs, which means whether they pay enough to raise a family on, should be central. This means the Democratic Party should become the party that works to restore America's industry and manufacturing. If that brings free trade into question, so be it; Democrats can leave free trade to the Republicans. Most voters would rather have good jobs than free trade.

* Restrictions on immigration and on out-sourcing jobs overseas. Immigration and out-sourcing are the two biggest threats to jobs middle and lower-middle class Americans need.

* A pro-growth policy on population, which means the Democrats would once again favor large families. On abortion, the Democrats would say abortion should be legal but rare and mean it. The best way to do that is to adopt the "95/10 Plan" promoted by Democrats for Life, which says that within ten years we should provide alternatives to abortion in 95% of all cases.

* Instead of the "multiculturalism" demanded by cultural Marxism, the Democratic Party should once again become the party of racial integration, which means acculturating blacks and immigrants into standard middle-class American values. That is the only way blacks and immigrants can hope to become members of the middle class economically. Movements such as that to make English America's official language should be welcomed and supported by the Democratic Party as ways to help its minority con-

stituents.

The fact that we are recommending these positions to the Democratic Party does not mean we agree with all of them. We believe abortion should be against the law.

But a platform such as this could make the Democratic Party a potential majority party once more, which would be helpful in restoring the republic. The toughest challenge for the Democrats will be showing cultural Marxism the door, because so much of their party's money comes from elites that hate traditional American culture and the Christian religion. The Democrats face a choice: that money or the votes of average Americans.

A restored republic may seem like an impossible dream in the face of Leviathan, the vast imperial government in Washington. But it must be a central goal of the next conservatism. So long as Washington remains nothing more than a rich feeding ground for the New Class, the crisis of legitimacy of the American state will grow. Eventually, that crisis will break on us with terrible force, leading to internal disorder of the kind we see in too many parts of the world. That is not the future we want to leave to our grandchildren.

Chapter Three

Winning the War for Western Culture

At the heart of the challenge facing conservatives lies one simple fact: while we focused our efforts on politics, our opponents on the left focused on the culture.

Each of us won. We elected lots of Republicans, most of whom pretended to be conservatives (a few actually were). Grass-roots conservatives moved the Republican Party out of what seemed to be permanent minority status, first to capturing the White House and then to controlling both Houses of Congress. That was political victory on a grand scale.

Unfortunately, the left won an equally large victory over our culture. What was called the "counter-culture" in the 1960s — cultural Marxism — now controls almost every aspect of our society: the entertainment industry (the most powerful cultural force in America), music, fine arts, the media, the universities, the public schools, even many churches. Cultural Marxism is using these institutions to achieve its purpose, the destruction of traditional Western culture and the Christian religion. All we have to do is look around us and compare what we see with the America of the 1950s to understand how vast the left's victory has been. The old sins have become virtues and the old virtues have become sins.

The nub of the problem is this: culture is stronger than

politics. Despite everything conservatives have achieved in politics, the left's cultural victory trumps our political victories. That is why even when we win election after election, our country continues to deteriorate.

The next conservatism must have winning the culture war as its main theme. Conservatives have already taken some important steps toward doing so. Starting in the mid-1980s when the Free Congress Foundation introduced cultural conservatism, more and more elements of the conservative movement have come to realize that if we lose the culture war, we also lose everything else. Culture is no longer at the periphery of conservatives' concerns, although it may not yet be at the center where it needs to be.

The question is, how can we win this war? The rest of this chapter, and much of the rest of this book, is devoted to addressing that question. We do not claim to offer a complete answer, nor a magic formula. We have some ideas to suggest, and a strategy. We propose a way forward, expecting that others will also have ideas to offer, some no doubt better than ours.

Of one thing we are certain: unless the next conservatism has a strategy that offers a realistic hope of reversing conservatism's cultural defeat and restoring our country to its rightful mind, it will not be worth calling "the next conservatism." Reversing the decline, decay and seemingly bottomless degradation of America's culture must be recognized as conservatism's most urgent and most difficult challenge in any new conservative agenda.

Cultural Marxism

Where should we start? Since this is a war, a good starting point might be a maxim of the famous Chinese military theorist Sun Tzu, who lived some 2,000 years ago and whose writings are widely respected still. Sun Tzu wrote, "He who knows himself and knows his enemy will win 100 battles."

We have just summed up conservatives' situation: political victories but cultural defeat. What do we know about our enemy?

America's cultural implosion did not just "happen." It is the product of a conscious effort to destroy Western culture that goes back to World War I. We have already noted that the ideology that effort created, commonly known as "Political Correctness" or "multiculturalism," is really cultural Marxism. But if we are to know our enemy, we have to know where it came from. A short history lesson is in order, on the history of cultural Marxism.

Cultural Marxism began not in the 1960s but in 1919, immediately after World War I. Marxist theory had predicted that in the event of a major war in Europe, the working class all over the continent would rise up to overthrow capitalism and create Communism. But when war broke out in 1914, that did not happen. On the contrary, the workers in every European country put on their uniforms and marched off to slaughter each other in the millions, in the name of nationalism. When a Marxist revolution did succeed in Russia in 1917, workers in other European countries did not support it. What had gone wrong?

Independently, two Marxist theorists, Antonio Gramsci in Italy and Georg Lukacs in Hungary, came up with the same answer: Western culture and the Christian religion had so blinded the working class to its "true," Marxist class interests that Communism was impossible in the West until both could be destroyed. In 1919, Lukacs asked, "Who will save us from Western civilization?" That same year, when he became Deputy Commissar for Culture in the short-lived Bolshevik Bela Kun government in Hungary, one of Lukacs's first acts was to introduce sex education into

Hungary's public schools. He knew that if he could destroy the West's traditional sexual morals, he would have taken a giant step toward destroying Western culture itself.

In 1923, inspired in part by Lukacs, a group of German Marxists established a think tank at Frankfurt University in Germany called the Institute for Social Research. This institute, soon known simply as the Frankfurt School, would become the creator of cultural Marxism, aka "Political Correctness."

To translate Marxism from economic into cultural terms, the members of the Frankfurt School – Max Horkheimer, Theodor Adorno, Wilhelm Reich, Erich Fromm and Herbert Marcuse, to name the most important – had to contradict Marx (and Moscow) on several points. They argued that culture was not just part of what Marx had called society's "superstructure," but an independent and very important variable. They also said that the working class would not lead a Marxist revolution, because it was becoming part of the middle class, the evil bourgeoisie.

Who would? In the 1950s, Herbert Marcuse answered the question: a coalition of blacks, students, Feminist women and homosexuals, the "victims" groups Political Correctness prates about endlessly.

Fatefully for America, when Hitler came to power in Germany in 1933, the Frankfurt School fled – and reestablished itself in New York City with help from Columbia University. There, it shifted its focus from destroying Western culture in Germany to destroying it in the United States, the country that had given it refuge.

To do so, the Frankfurt School invented "Critical Theory," which is something of a play on words. What is the theory? The theory is to criticize, subjecting every traditional institution, starting with the family, to brutal and unremitting criticism in order to bring them down. Critical

Theory in turn creates a climate of "cultural pessimism," in which all traditions, no matter how well they may function, are seen as having something deeply wrong with them.

To Critical Theory and cultural pessimism, the Frankfurt School added yet another culturally destructive weapon: its series of publications called "studies in prejudice," which culminated in Theodor Adorno's immensely influential book *The Authoritarian Personality*, published in 1950. These works said that anyone who believes in and lives by traditional Western culture is evil, a "racist" or "sexist" or "fascist" – and is also mentally ill.

The question facing the members of the Frankfurt School was, how could they couple their culturally destructive philosophy with a weapon powerful enough to actually destroy Western culture? They knew philosophy alone was too weak. Fatefully, they hit on a brilliant answer. Crossing Marx with Freud, they took from psychology a tool known as "psychological conditioning." By endless repetition, psychological conditioning works ideas directly into the unconscious, without any need for rational argument. The Frankfurt School worked psychological conditioning that transmitted their cultural Marxism into education theory, into the mass media and into the entertainment industry (Horkheimer and Adorno spent the war years in Hollywood).

After World War II, most members of the Frankfurt School went back to Germany. But Herbert Marcuse stayed in America. He took the highly abstract philosophical works of other Frankfurt School members and repackaged them in ways college students could read and understand. In his book *Eros and Civilization* he argued that by freeing sex from any restraints we could elevate the "pleasure principle" over the "reality principle" and create a society with no work, just play (Marcuse coined the phrase, "Make love, not war"). Marcuse also argued for what he called "liberating tolerance," which he defined as tolerance for all ideas coming from the left and intolerance for any ideas coming from the right (this is what university leftists mean when they call for "tolerance"). In the 1960s, Marcuse became the chief "guru" of the New Left, and he injected the cultural Marxism of the Frankfurt School into the Baby Boom generation, to the point where it is now America's unofficial state ideology.

The next conservatism must unmask multiculturalism and Political Correctness and tell the American people what they really are: cultural Marxism, whose goal remains what Lukacs and Gramsci set in 1919: destroying Western culture and the Christian religion (more the irony that it is prominent in so many churches). It has already made vast strides toward that goal. But if the average American found out that Political Correctness is a form of Marxism – different from the Marxism of the old Soviet Union, but Marxism nonetheless – it would be in serious trouble. It would quickly lose its claim to the moral high ground. The next conservatism must reveal the man behind the curtain – old Karl Marx himself.

We encourage readers to go beyond this short history of cultural Marxism and study the threat it poses in more detail. Free Congress Foundation has produced a video documentary on the Frankfurt School, "The History of Political Correctness," which you can find on Google. The Free Congress website offers a book on cultural Marxism, "Political Correctness: A Short History of an Ideology," which is available at http://www.freecongress.org/centers.cc/index.aspx. You are welcome to make and distribute as many copies of that book as you wish. In includes an annotated bibliography of further readings. Of particular value is Lorenz Jäger's excellent new biography, *Adorno*.

Brave New World

The road down which cultural Marxism is leading America is all too clear. It is the road to Brave New World.

When the authors of this volume were in high school, which was some years ago, every pupil had to read two books which warned about two alternative totalitarian futures. One was George Orwell's *1984*, which represented the totalitarianism of Stalin's Soviet Union. The other was a slim novel, written in the 1930s by the British author Aldous Huxley: *Brave New World*. If the fall of the Soviet Union removed most of the threat of *1984* (at least outside the domain of the Department of Homeland Security), America is today steering straight for Brave New World. Indeed, it is leading the rest of the planet in that direction, or, where necessary, forcing it by invasion (ironically under the code word of "freedom").

The first law in Huxley's *Brave New World* was that you must be happy. Happiness was guaranteed, or compelled, by a combination of sensual and sexual pleasure (as with Marcuse, anything goes, except marriage), endless consumerism and materialism, entertainment through virtual realities (the "feelies" did television and computer games one better), psychological conditioning and, Hell's final triumph, genetic conditioning, which was virtually inescapable. In its totality, *Brave New World* represents what C.S. Lewis called the "abolition of man."

The next conservatism should recognize that *Brave New World* describes America's probable future, unless conservatives, perhaps in coalition with others who recognize the danger, can bring about a massive change in direction. All the key elements are already present and working as a leaven throughout American society, save only genetic conditioning, and genetic engineering will soon give us that.

40

The question facing the next conservatism is what can be done about it. Concrete steps include home or other private schooling and throwing the television off the roof, as Russell Kirk once actually did. Many of the ideas presented subsequently in this chapter are intended to offer escapes from Brave New World. Other potentially effective counteractions include:

* Make sure every school child, and every adult who has not done so, reads Huxley's *Brave New World*. It offers a powerful warning.
* Beware of psychological conditioning in any form ("sensitivity training" is a common one, and many public schools now do little but psychologically condition), and fight genetic engineering with all our power.
* Recognize that cultural Marxism, while not the same thing as Brave New World, has made a Devil's pact with it, where each uses and benefits the other. Conservatives should be fighting both.

One of the next conservatism's most challenging tasks is to reverse Marcuse and restore the reality principle in place of the pleasure principle. If we do not, events will, and those events are not likely to be pleasant.

Race and Sex

In the fight against cultural Marxism, there are two issues some conservatives may wish to avoid. Those issues are race and sex, or "gender" as the cultural Marxists would have it (as conservatives, we think sex is better than gender). The cultural Marxists have sought to make any views on these subjects other than their own "toxic," which means they dare not be spoken. Cultural Marxism argues that only blacks can say anything about the race issue, and they are only allowed to spout the party line. It defines any conservative black, or any black who adheres to standard middle-class values, as "white." It says the same thing about "women's issues." Only Feminist women are allowed to have a say.

Poppycock. The next conservatism must have the courage to walk up to cultural Marxism's clay idol and break off its nose. As conservatives, we cannot ignore America's race problem. Nor can blacks, who suffer more than anyone else from the failure of past policies.

Here as elsewhere, the next conservatism attempts to look down the road and see where we want to end up in the future. Our starting point should be a realization that the civil rights era is over. The main problem facing American blacks is not white racism or unfair discrimination. In fact, under "affirmative action" it is whites and Asians who are discriminated against. The main problem facing blacks is a cultural breakdown within the urban black community, a breakdown that has had tragic effects in terms of crime, drug use, illegitimacy, abortion and an unwillingness of too many young blacks to get a good education so they can join the American middle class.

Ironically, it is the values preached by the cultural Marxists in the 1960s that brought about this breakdown. People such as Herbert Marcuse preached a culture of instant gratification: "If it feels good, do it." Middle-class white kids "did it" in college, then went on to law school or business school and successful middle-class lives. In the ghetto, black kids just kept on doing it, resulting in the sort of values we hear in rap music and see in action in our inner cities. It has been an enormous national tragedy, one that has wasted countless lives.

It is important that we, as conservatives, remind ourselves and other Americans that it was not always like this.

The black inner city of 50 or 60 years ago was not a bad place. It was largely poor, and many blacks did then suffer from racial prejudice, which was wrong. But the black community of that time was not disordered. It was not unsafe. The problems in black schools were the same as problems in white schools, running in the halls and talking in class. Children were not shot and killed on their way to or from school for their jacket or their shoes or because they looked at someone else's girl. As late as the 1950s, 80% of black children came home from school to a married mother and father. If you were white, you could walk through those neighborhoods in safety. The people you met there would be friendly toward you.

Fortunately, some courageous black leaders are beginning to defy cultural Marxism and address the real issues. They are pointing out to other blacks that the black community's current problems are a result of blacks' own behavior. They are condemning the culture of instant gratification that has poisoned the black community. They are telling their own people that they must recover their old culture where the black church was strong and blacks, like whites, adhered to solid middle class values, which start with delayed gratification. For blacks, whites, and everyone else, middle-class values work best.

This ties in directly with the next conservatism's rejection of multiculturalism. We recognize that America needs to have one common culture. That culture must be based on middle-class values that begin with delayed gratification and include the merit of hard work, education, saving, lifetime marriage and working your way up in the world. Again, these were values the black community shared with whites only a few decades back. No one has ever known more sincere, self-sacrificing Christians than the "church ladies" who were the backbone of the old black community.

The next conservatism's position on race needs two elements. First, we will not fall for the line that America's racial problem is white racism. That was true once to some degree, but it is not true now. Most whites wish blacks well.

Second, we must support in any way we can the black community's efforts to recover from its own cultural collapse. It is vital for blacks and whites alike that blacks, especially black young people, recover the middle class values of their grandparents. The same is of course true for young whites, Hispanics and Asians (it is precisely these values, which are strongly paralleled by Confucian values, that enable east Asians to do so well in America).

The next conservatism's goal should be the same as the goal of the civil-rights movement of the 1940s and 1950s: an America where skin color is merely incidental because almost everyone lives solid, middle-class lives.

Feminism

Just as cultural Marxism has used blacks as a weapon to destroy our traditional culture, greatly damaging the black community in the process, so it has also used and harmed women. Feminism is much older than cultural Marxism, and 19th century Feminism often sought to defend the family through reforms such as the family wage, which paid a higher wage to a male head of household so his wife and children could stay home instead of working (labor law now forbids a family wage as "discrimination").

Sadly, today's Feminism is almost entirely controlled by cultural Marxists. They use Feminism as a tool to destroy the traditional family, an institution which greatly benefits women. As rates of divorce and illegitimacy attest, they have had too much success, with women their main victims. How many aging baby boomer women, who welcomed Feminism when they were young, now wish, too late, that they could have the lives their grandmothers lived?

To understand the threat Feminism poses to our traditional culture, the next conservatism needs to consider the matter more deeply than conservatives have done in the past.[1]

A critical change in the left over the last few decades has been the shift from the economic to the social and increasingly the sexual. What was once a semi-socialistic attack on property and enterprise has become a social and sexual attack on the family, marriage, and masculinity.

The consequences are incalculable. No ideology in human history has been potentially so invasive of the private sphere of life as Feminism. Communists had little respect for privacy. Feminists have made it their main target.

Like other radical movements, only more so, Feminism's danger comes not so much from the assault on freedom (which traditional tyrannies also threaten) but specifically from the attack on private life, especially family life (which traditional dictatorships usually leave alone). "Radical Feminism is totalitarian because it denies the individual a private space; every private thought and action is public and, therefore, political," writes Robert Bork. "The party or the movement claims the right to control every aspect of life."

The left's brilliant move has been to clothe its attack on the family as a defense of "women and children." Marian Wright Edelman openly acknowledges she founded the Children's Defense Fund to push a leftist agenda: "I got the

---

1 The following discussion of Feminism was contributed by Steven Baskerville, president of the American Coalition for Fathers and Children.

idea that children might be a very effective way to broaden the base for change." This climaxed in the Clinton administration, where radical policy innovations were invariably justified as "for the children." Using children to leverage an expansion of state power by eliminating family privacy is succinctly conveyed in Hillary Clinton's aphorism, "There is no such thing as other people's children."

This nationalization of the family under the guise of protecting it leaves pro-family politicians in a difficult position. One way out is to join in the demonization of those who literally embody the Feminists' hated "patriarchy": fathers. Relabeled "deadbeat dads," "batterers," and "pedophiles," fathers are now railroaded into jail through methods one recent scholar, writing in the *Rutgers Law Review*, calls a "due process fiasco," and Bryce Christensen says is leading to a "police state."

Knee-jerk calls to "get tough" on criminals have unintended consequences when the penal apparatus has been commandeered by Feminists, who redefine criminality to include an assortment of gender offenses that bear little relation to what most Americans understand as crime.

The evolution of the Justice Department's Office of Victims of Crime illustrates the deception. Proceeding from President Reagan's 1982 Task Force on Victims of Crime, this agency has since been hijacked by Feminists, and most of the "crimes" have been redefined in Feminist terms. By definition, the "victims" are all women, the "perpetrators" are all men, and the "crimes" are mostly political: sexual harassment, date "rape" (which is seldom rape), domestic "violence" (that is not violent), child abuse (that may be ordinary parental discipline), "stalking" (fathers trying to see their children), and so forth.

Far from softening the hard edges of male-dominated power politics, Feminism has inserted calculations of power into the most private corners of life and subjected family life to bureaucratic control. This is what makes the dream of a more "caring" public sphere through Feminism not only naïve but dangerously utopian. For as Feminists correctly pointed out, the feminine functions were traditionally private; politicizing the feminine has therefore meant politicizing private life. This is why the "totalitarian" potential which Bork senses is already being realized.

"All politics is on one level sexual politics," writes George Gilder. At least sexual politics is the logical culmination of all *radical politics*, which is the politics that has defined modern history. More than any other threat, Feminism demands that the next conservatism examine conservatives' own reflexes and habits in a world where radical assumptions have permeated well beyond the ranks of leftist ideologues. It demands that a new conservative agenda challenge not just this doctrine or that, but the very concept of a politics defined by ideologies, activists, organizations, opinion-mongers, and a professional political class for whom politics is all-consuming. The next conservatism must try to recover a civic life of citizens, householders, parents, churches and synagogues, local communities, and values that transcend political calculation. Czech dissident and later president Vaclav Havel called this "apolitical politics": a world where, contrary to Feminists, cultural Marxists and all ideologues, the personal is not political.

Retroculture

Thus far in this chapter, we have identified some of the most powerful forces working to destroy our traditional Western culture. We have suggested some tactics for countering those threats. But wars cannot be won merely through good tactics. The next conservatism needs a new strategy.

The strategy we recommend is Retroculture. What

Retroculture means is that in our own lives and the lives of our families, and perhaps eventually our communities, we would consciously, deliberately revive old ways of living. Of course, we would not exactly recreate the past. But we would use the past as a guide and a benchmark.

We realize this is a radical proposal. It is not a call for nostalgia. Nostalgia is merely an emotion, a wistful longing for what may be an imaginary past. Retroculture is concrete, and it is about action, not emotion. It calls for reshaping our lives to resemble, on a broad scale, the lives our forefathers led.

We know this runs counter to most of America's history. From the Pilgrims onward, America was always future-focused. Almost all Americans believed that the present was better than the past, and the future would be better than the present.

That has changed. In January, 1992, more than fifteen years ago, Free Congress Foundation sponsored a national survey of attitudes toward the past. The sample was 1,000 registered voters throughout the United States, and the survey was conducted by Lawrence Research, a respected polling firm.

The results were astonishing: 49% of those surveyed said that life was better in the past than it is today; only 17% said it was worse. Specific aspects of life a majority said were better in the past included our economy (62%), our moral values (74%), our environment (66%), our community and family life (70%), our pace of life (64%), the quality of services (51%), the quality of workmanship (57%) and loyalty of employees to their companies or corporations (59%). Forty-seven percent of those surveyed felt their grandparents were happier than they are. Only 29% said they were not as happy.

When given a choice of six times and places in which

they would prefer to live, a majority of 58% chose a typical suburb in 1950. In last place with just 6% was Los Angeles in 1991. When asked for a second choice, a plurality of 32% chose a small town in 1900.

When asked their opinion of the Victorian period, when the middle-class society we had up through the 1950s was created, 56% had a favorable opinion, 30% unfavorable. 61% said that life in the 1950s was better than life today.

Forty-five percent said they see signs of people and things turning back toward the past, and find that a good thing. Only 7% said it was a bad thing. Fifty-nine percent said they thought our political leaders should be trying to lead the nation back toward the way we used to be.

The results of this survey suggest that America is no longer future-focused. Public opinion is ready for Retroculture. Millions of Americans might rally to a call to return to the ways in which we used to live.

Brave New World, which hates the past and attempts to demonize it, tells us, "You can't go back." Why not? It only makes sense that what worked then can work now. That might not be a bad slogan for a Retroculture movement. It is true in so many areas of our lives. It is true about families, marriage and sexual morals; finance, both family and national (everybody used to know that debt is dangerous); entertainment, which used to be both good and decent; even in areas such as transportation, where streetcars were better than buses and, in cities, better than cars.

Through Retroculture, the next conservatism should seek to rebuild our old culture from the bottom up, one individual or family at a time. That is slow. But there is no other way to win the culture war. We have lost so much ground since the 1960s that we almost have to start all over again. When it comes to our culture, it is too late to conserve. We have to restore.

Cultural restoration should not be, indeed cannot be, imposed through political power. To try to do so would run counter to the next conservatism's call to restore the republic. A true republic keeps power in check. It understands that Tolkien's ring of power is power itself, which in the long run cannot be used for good. The only safe form of power is power of example. That is how the restoration of our traditional culture through Retroculture must proceed, bottom-up, person by person and family by family, on a voluntary basis.

The restoration movement in architecture shows how Retroculture works. In the 1960s and 1970s, it was fashionable among architects and urban planners to rip down Victorian and even colonial buildings and put up new ones. The new ones were usually awful. Now, most people agree that older buildings can and should be restored rather than replaced, even if they serve new purposes.

In the rest of this chapter, we will look at a number of aspects of American life through the lens of Retroculture, the recovery of old ways and their restoration as part of modern life. We begin with an old conservative virtue, one coming from the same root (in more ways than one) as the word "conservative:" conservation.

Conservation

The next conservatism should regard environmentalism warily. It is on the verge of becoming an ideology, if it is not one already. It is potentially the most radically anti-human of all ideologies. Some environmentalists already call man a "cancer" on the planet, suggesting the earth would be a paradise if only man were eliminated. Exactly who would enjoy this paradise is hard to say; presumably, cockroaches and crows.

But conservation is another matter. As conservatives,

we believe in conserving many things: traditions, morals and culture, but also clean air and water, farms and countryside, energy (much of which now must be imported) and the soil itself, on which we all depend for our daily bread.

Conservatives do not like waste. Reckless, frivolous, thoughtless consumption was never a conservative virtue. Like many conservatives, the authors of this book grew up in households where nothing was wasted. We used everything until it was used up, or until we passed it on to other people who needed it more than we did. We seldom bought things we did not need. That is a good way to live, regardless of how much money we have. A society's real strength comes from production, saving and investment, not consumption. Earlier generations of Americans understood this and lived accordingly.

Conservation needs to be part of the next conservatism. This will become all the more important as energy becomes more expensive, and some traditional sources of energy such as oil become relatively scarce.

But there is a larger aspect to conservation, one that ties into a central idea of the next conservatism: the importance of local life. Globalism, which is a handmaiden of Brave New World, preaches bigness. We are told we must welcome a "world economy" where virtually all our manufactured goods come from overseas, our energy comes from massive international corporations, our food from huge agribusinesses. The Globalists seldom talk about how vulnerable this leaves us to events in other parts of the world. Nor do they speak of the consequences for the lives of ordinary Americans, who are left both dependent on and in competition with other peoples all over the world. Globalism averages America's economy and standard of living with those of places such as India and China. That means they move up, but we move down.

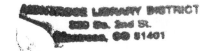

The next conservatism's conservation should point away from Globalism and toward a renewed focus on local life. Our forefathers' lives, for the most part, were lived locally. An Amish friend of Mr. Lind says, "The reason we use buggies is that we want life to be local."

Some new technologies may be helpful here. In the future, it may be possible to produce most energy locally, from solar or wind power or in-home fuel cells. Even with current technology, there is a great deal we can do to reduce our dependence on big systems by reviving old ways. In much of America, we can eat food grown locally, including in our own garden, and use local products more than most of us do now. Often, the quality is better, and if the price is somewhat higher, the money is going to our neighbors rather than to some international mega-corporation.

There are two conservation movements the next conservatism should support strongly: sustainable agriculture and organic farming. Both attempt to restore and maintain the fertility of the soil itself, as opposed to relying on ever greater doses of chemicals (mostly derived from imported petroleum) and genetically engineered crops. America's fertile soil is perhaps our most important natural resource, one we should feel honor bound as good stewards to pass on in a healthy condition to future generations. Sustainable agriculture and organic farming, in turn, tie into efforts to promote local food through farmer's markets and cooperatives and to restore family farming as a viable way of life.

We have suggested that "think locally, act locally" needs to be a principle of the next conservatism if we want to steer our country away from Brave New World. Conservation, in turn, is a necessary part of thinking and acting locally, because if we do not conserve our local land, water and air we foul our own neighborhood.

As conservatives, we should not fall for environmentalism

or any other ideology. But we should conserve, in the ways we live our own lives. We can then serve as examples to the people around us. The next conservatism, like all real conservatism, is ultimately a way of life.

Agrarianism

Conservation of land, water and air points us to another Retroculture way of life, agrarianism. Earlier generations of conservatives were agrarians. They thought life on a family farm was a good life. It built strong families and communities, communities where faith could flourish and community expectations reinforced sound morals. We believe that is still true. Bringing back the family farm as a viable way of life should be an important component of the next conservatism.

Some people may object that such a program is simply not possible. Brave New World tells us the family farm cannot be economically viable in today's world – despite the steady rise in agricultural commodity prices created by Globalism.

Experience says otherwise. A growing number of Americans are earning decent incomes from family farms. Mr. Lind's Amish friend, David Kline, who is the editor of *Farming* magazine, raises 30 to 40 dairy cows on about 140 acres. His cows, which graze in pastures eight months out of the year even in Ohio's climate, give him an annual income of about $75,000. Most of the cows' feed for the winter also comes from his farm, where a good year often gives him 200 bushels of corn per acre. Because he farms organically, buying no chemical fertilizers, herbicides or pesticides, his expenses are small. His farm, Larksong, is a beautiful place, its well-tended fields alight with bluebirds and butterflies.

The next conservatism needs to be willing to learn from

others. One place to start is with the Amish. The Amish are cultural conservatives. They live according to the beliefs most conservatives espouse: Christian faith, strong families, close-knit communities where people can and do depend on each other, communities based in the church. The Amish are also successful practitioners of Retroculture. If their buggies had bumper stickers, one might read, "We know what Jesus would drive."

The next conservatism can also learn from the organic farming movement. Many people, including some conservatives, want organic products and are willing to pay a premium for them. That helps the farmer receive a fair price for his products, one that makes his farm viable. The workman is worthy of his hire.

As conservatives, we should not see cheapness as the highest virtue. That is the mindset of commercialism, not conservatism. Russell Kirk wrote, "So America's contribution to the universal "democratic capitalism" of the future . . . will be just this: cheapness, the cheapest music and the cheapest comic-books and the cheapest morality that can be provided." He might have added the cheapest agricultural products, regardless of what that does to agrarian life. That is not the direction in which the next conservatism should go.

Agriculture and agrarian life are a whole culture, not just a way to make a living, and we should seek to protect that culture and make it available to more families. A recent article in *Farming* magazine (a publication we would recommend to readers of this book), "Conversations with the Land" by Jim Van Der Pol, gave insight into that culture:

> Recently I sat in a church mourning the passage of another farmer from a world that can ill afford to spare even one. I thought of Leonard's love of farmer talk . . . the telling again of stories connected

with people and places in a long and well lived human life. . . .

"See," he would tell me after naming all the farmers who have exchanged work together in his circle, "nobody ever kept track of who spent how much time doing things for which others. Everyone just figured it would work out. It always did."

Leonard was in his farming and his life a maker of art, a husband to his wife and his farm, a human creating in the context of Creation itself. . . .

Beyond promoting the family farm, the next conservatism should seek to make the countryside available to as many Americans as possible. The Mennonites have a wonderful program where they bring inner-city children to their farms for part of their summer vacations. What a tremendous and life-giving change for kids who have never known anything but asphalt and video games and crime! Many cities and towns now have farmer's markets where people in the city and suburbs can buy fresh farm products directly from the farmers. Both the farmers and the city-dwellers benefit.

The next conservatism should look toward a world where, as Tolkien put it, there is less noise and more green. Our goal should be to make agrarian life, in all its dimensions, available to as many Americans as possible, both those who farm for their living and those who earn their incomes in other ways but want a tie to the countryside. In this respect, the next conservatism should be like an older conservatism we seem to have forgotten. Conservatives should become agrarians again.

Materialism

Some people who call themselves conservatives may sneer

that few family farmers get rich. Frankly, we find strange the idea that materialism, the notion that goodness or happiness come from owning ever more stuff, is conservative. Vast, ugly McMansions, hulking SUVs, households that have more cars than people, the latest and most expensive of everything (most of it acquired by piling up debt) are now supposedly signs that the nominal owners are conservatives. Each party, it seems, has adopted its characteristic vice as a virtue: for liberals, lust, and for conservatives, gluttony.

Earlier generations of conservatives would have been appalled by this mis-labeling. Conservatives looked down upon crass materialism and conspicuous consumption as marks of the *nouveau riche* and the snob. Happiness, conservatives knew, came not from piling up stuff but from doing the duties of one's station, with little thought of material reward.

No binge runs on forever, and as mountains of debt come crashing down, the next conservatism will need to put materialism back in its rightful place. A passage in Wendell Berry's novel *A World Lost* offers a view of materialism that may be genuinely conservative:

> Dick and Aunt Sarah Jane's two-room house at the edge of the woods, down the hill from the barns, was a part of the Home Place, but it was also a place unto itself, with its own garden and henhouse and woodpile. . . . She kept house and cared for a small flock of chickens and foraged in the fields and woods and sewed and mended and read her Bible. In the mornings and the evenings and in odd times spared from the farmwork, Dick kept their house supplied with water and milk, meat and firewood. I remember their pleasure in all the items of their small abundance. . . .

A "small abundance," abundance in the little things that make day-to-day life comfortable, is consistent with the conservative virtues. A small abundance implies no competition with one's neighbors, no ostentation, nor any wastefulness. One may take pleasure in such abundance without shame or guilt. It is an abundance open even to the poor, which Dick and Aunt Sarah Jane were by common measure.

The notion of a small abundance points to a broader concept that may also be conservative, namely an intensive rather than an extensive valuation of material things. Previous generations placed a higher value on possessing a few things of good quality than on lots of "store-bought stuff." These items lasted for generations and took on meaning from each generation that owned and used them. People did not throw out their furniture every ten years and buy new. They valued the familiar over the "latest thing," the worn, hand-woven rug over cheap new carpeting, Grandma's black walnut kitchen table over flashy granite countertops. It now seems that the more ostentatious the kitchen, the less food gets cooked in it.

Because genuine conservatism values the past and seeks to learn from it, these older attitudes toward material things can be guideposts for us. They point us away from the wild materialism of recent years (one visitor to America, a Hollander, said, "Americans are just Pac-man with legs"), not toward asceticism, but toward that small abundance and deep appreciation of good, old things our grandparents enjoyed. Things can have meaning, but they do not acquire their meaning from their price tags, nor from Martha Stewart. Their meaning grows from the skill and love the craftsman put into their making, and from the generations of people, known to us or unknown, in whose lives they played a part. Such material things, like people, have memory.

Crunchy Cons

Some of the themes we have suggested ought to be part of the next conservatism – agrarianism, conservation, re-evaluation of materialism – were recently brought together in a book by columnist and former writer for *National Review* Rod Dreher. The title of the book is *Crunchy Cons*, a reference to conservatives who eat granola, itself a symbol of a simpler life. We find the title unfortunate, as it suggests a "pop culture" phenomenon (titles, we know, are often thrust on helpless authors by their publishers). But we think the next conservatism should welcome "crunchy cons," right along with the Fiber One cons so many of us have become.

What the book *Crunchy Cons* advocates is not something new and shallow but something old and deep, the traditionalist conservatism of Russell Kirk. Dreher is familiar with Kirk's writings, and rightly argues that his understanding of conservatism is important to the renewal of the conservative movement.

Dreher offers a "Crunchy Cons Manifesto" other conservatives may find thoughtful. Its points include:

* Modern conservatism has become too focused on money, power, and the accumulation of stuff.
* Big business deserves as much skepticism as big government.
* Culture is more important than politics and economics.
* Small, Local, Old and Particular are almost always better than Big, Global, New and Abstract.
* Beauty is more important than efficiency.
* The relentlessness of media-driven pop culture deadens our senses to authentic truth, beauty and wisdom.

✳ We share Russell Kirk's conviction that "the institution most essential to conserve is the family."

One of the questions *Crunchy Cons* raises is just how important efficiency and even economics itself should be to conservatives. Dreher writes, "we can't build anything good unless we live by the belief that man does not exist to serve the economy, but the economy exists to serve man." The next conservatism wants everyone to have the opportunity for a decent standard of living, but Dreher is correct in saying,

> A society built on consumerism must break down eventually for the same reason socialism did: because even though it is infinitely better than socialism at meeting our physical needs and gratifying our physical desires, consumerism also treats human beings as merely materialists, as ciphers on a spreadsheet. It cannot, over time, serve the deepest needs of the human person for stability, spirituality, and authentic community. We should not be surprised that it has led to social disintegration.

We can imagine Russell Kirk saying "Hear! Hear!" to this. Kirk would also agree with Dreher's rejection of relativism, not only in morals but also in aesthetics. Dreher writes,

> In his 1994 book *The Old Way of Seeing* . . . architect [Jonathan] Hale argued that the rampant charmlessness of our built environment is a function of America's loss of historical memory: "Everywhere in the buildings of the past is relationship among parts: contrast, tension, balance. Compare the buildings of today and we see no such patterns. We see fragmentation, mismatched systems, uncertainty.

This disintegration tends to produce not ugliness so much as dullness . . .

In other words, there are canons of architecture and aesthetics, and they ought to be respected. The next conservatism, too, should talk about resurrecting old canons.

Dreher unfortunately falls prey to environmentalism, failing to perceive it as a new and dangerous ideology. But he is correct in saying conservatives ought also to be conservationists. He quotes powerfully from Pope John Paul II's encyclical *Centesimus Annus*:

> In his desire to have and to enjoy rather than to be and to grow, man consumes the resources of the earth and his own life in an excessive and disordered way. At the root of the senseless destruction of the natural environment lies an anthropological error, which unfortunately is widespread in our day. Man, who discovers his capacity to transform and in a certain sense create the world through his own work, forgets that this is always based on God's prior and original gift of the things that are. Man thinks that he can make arbitrary use of the earth, subjecting it without restraint to his own will, as though it did not have its own requisites and a prior God-given purpose, which man can indeed develop but must not betray. Instead of carrying out his role as a cooperator with God in the work of creation, man sets himself up in place of God and thus ends up provoking a rebellion on the part of nature, which is more tyrannized than governed by him.

Dreher is a Roman Catholic, but we think these words of the late Pope speak thoughtfully to all Christians.

New Urbanism

Thus far we have said a good deal about the countryside. But what about America's cities? Just as the next conservatism desires a thriving countryside, so it also should want thriving cities. Here, a new movement should be of interest to the next conservatism, a movement deeply rooted in Retroculture. It is called the New Urbanism.

The New Urbanism seeks to build new neighborhoods, villages and towns similar to those we built through most of America's history, up until World War II. It wants to revitalize our inner cities as well, again by returning them to the way they used to be. While New Urbanism does not always demand traditional architecture, it usually favors it. New Urbanism offers a Retroculture alternative to post-war sprawl suburbs, where everything looks the same and you cannot do anything without driving.

One of the New Urbanism's founders, architect Andres Duany, offers this more specific definition of New Urbanism:

> The New Urbanism can be described as a movement that fosters human communities that are, so far as the market will support, compact, connected, complete and convivial.
>
> 1. Compact in order to allow walkability. A resident's ordinary daily needs should be available within walking distance. These would include an elementary school, a grocery and general store, recreational and meeting places. Residents should not have to own an automobile in order to survive.
>
>   Compactness also conserves open space,

particularly places of beauty and spaces for recreation, and also land that can be farmed. Food self-sufficiency is an ideal, though it will seldom be attained in practice.

2. Connected by a variety of choices of transportation: walking, bicycles, cars and transit, preferably electric streetcars.

3. Complete in that each community should contain a range of housing types, suitable for a variety of people, including the next generation. Each should also contain a variety of shops and workplaces. Its setting should be such that it can become agriculturally self-sufficient in basic produce.

4. Convivial in that the public spaces of the community should be safe, participatory and enjoyable. People should be able to know their neighbors.

Conservatives should, we think, find all of these things acceptable, so long as suburban sprawl also remains an option for those who prefer it. We do not want New Urbanism mandated by government, any more than we want sprawl mandated by government – as is now the case.

But the reason why we think New Urbanism should have an honored place in the next conservative agenda goes beyond questions of architecture and urban design to a more important subject, namely how life is lived in neighborhoods, villages and towns (and traditional neighborhoods within cities). Put simply, genuine community can grow more easily and develop more fully in those traditional places than in typical modern suburbs.

Why is that the case? Because in traditional neighborhoods we interact a lot with the people who live around us, while in conventional sprawl suburbs we usually do not. It is a cliché to say that people who live in sprawl suburbs do not know their neighbors, but it is often true. It is easy to see why by looking at a typical suburban day.

You get up in the morning, grab a quick cup of coffee and head out the door. But the door leads to your garage, not outside. You get in your car, open the garage door, turn on the radio and the air conditioning, and back out. You might, at most, wave to a neighbor in his car. You know where he lives but you do not know his name. Because you are both in automobiles, you could not stop and talk to him if you wanted to.

At work, you may be stuck in an office park, or on a strip center, unable to walk down a sidewalk for lunch with your co-workers.

Coming home in the evening, you do the same thing in reverse. If you stopped at a store or restaurant on the way, it was probably several miles from where you live. The other people there were drawn from a wide area. It is a rare occurrence to see anyone you know from your community.

Once home, you probably stay in the house. If you exercise, you drive to a gym. Most evenings you spend in front of the TV or the computer. You may go outside on weekends to cut the grass or barbeque, but most of what you or your kids do requires a trip in the car. You could not walk or ride a bike if you wanted to; the streets have no sidewalks and you would quickly come to a major road that has lots of fast traffic. It is not hard to understand why community seldom forms under these conditions. People have no places where they can meet their neighbors casually.

Contrast that suburban life to life in a traditional town, village or neighborhood. Grocery stores, shops, restaurants, churches, the library and the post office are all in walking distance. So at least is the elementary school, and maybe the high school as well. All streets have sidewalks, and a grid street pattern means you can always find a "back way" with less traffic if you want to walk or bicycle. Kids play outside in structured, supervised activities. To get to work, you may drive, but you may also walk to the bus or street-car stop.

All of these conditions draw people out of their houses and out of their cars. They spend a lot more time walking. Because the area is small and relatively self-contained, the people they meet live near them. They get to know their neighbors, which is the first step toward the formation of community. Unless that happens, community is impossible.

Why is community important? Because many conservative goals can best be attained in communities. The two things we want most to conserve are our traditional culture and our traditional morals. Conserving them means we must pass them on to the next generation, despite the best efforts of the surrounding "pop culture" to undermine them. We can pass them on much more effectively where they are supported by a community than when we have to try to teach them in isolation.

As anyone who has children knows, peer pressure is a powerful force with them (and with adults as well). When both adults and children live in a genuine community, the peer pressure to do the right thing instead of the wrong can be intense. It can be powerful enough to push back the deadly messages broadcast by the pop culture, which are the source of so many young people's downfall.

The role of the community in transmitting the culture to the next generation and upholding traditional morals for young and old alike is one of civilization's most ancient foundation stones. If that role goes unfilled, as it tends to do in sprawl suburbs where people do not know their neighbors, conservatism loses one of its strongest bulwarks. The next conservatism should include the New Urbanism not only because we want buildings to be handsome and cities to thrive. We need the New Urbanism because of the importance of community in winning the war for Western culture.

As it happens, there is a very conservative way in which the next conservatism can support the New Urbanism: by demanding a free market. All over the country, New Urbanist projects are selling well. The problem is, government regulations in the form of codes make it very difficult to build them.

Almost everywhere, the codes developers and builders are required by law to follow mandate sprawl. They require extreme single-use development, where residences, shops and workplaces are physically separated from each other by so much distance that you have to drive from one to another. A housing development cannot even include a coffee-house, a local restaurant or a small grocery.

To build according to New Urbanist principles, a private developer must get multiple variances, as many as three dozen for a small neighborhood. Each requires a process that takes both time and money. This is not the level playing-field a free market requires and conservatives want.

The next conservatism should demand fair play by advocating dual codes. A typical sprawl code would be retained, but a New Urbanist code would be added as an option. The developer or builder could choose to follow either one, depending on his estimate of what the market wants. That is how a free market is supposed to work.

It is worth our while to take a short look at how one type of New Urbanist code, called a "Smart Code," works. It embodies a principle the next conservatism may find useful in other contexts. That principle says, you may do or build anything you want, but not anywhere you want. There is a place for everything, and everything should be in its proper place.

The Smart Code is based on the Transect. The Transect identifies six zones:

* T-1: Natural. This is wilderness landscape with unbuilt private land and preserved land, such as parks and national or state forest.

* T-2: Rural. Mostly farms.

* T-3: Suburban. Big lots, plenty of green areas.

* T-4: General urban. A mix of individual houses, townhouses, small apartment buildings and some shops and small offices. Think of the old "streetcar suburbs."

* T-5: Urban center. Businesses, townhouses, large apartment buildings, civic buildings; most buildings are attached, as on a main road.

* T-6: Urban core. The city center, with tall buildings, almost all attached. Mostly commercial offices and stores.

There is also a provision for Special Districts, for heavy industry, stockyards and other functions that must be kept well away from residences.

The way the Smart Code works is very simple. It allows developers and builders to do what they want within the appropriate zone of the Transect. Somewhere within the Transect, a builder can build and a buyer can buy virtually anything.

Transportation

Just as a recovery of the past has much to offer us in architecture and urban planning, so it does in transportation as well. That may come as a surprise. Have gas prices gone so high we should go back to riding horses?

Not quite. Between travel by horse and travel by car, something else intervened: travel by rail. Trains, along with their city cousins, streetcars, offer a pleasant, energyefficient, enjoyable way to travel, between cities and within a city. We used to have lots of them. As late as the 1950s, it was possible to go from virtually anywhere in America to anywhere else in America, without a car and without flying.

Then someone took our trains and trolleys away. Who? The government, of course. As early as 1921, government – local, state and federal – was pouring more than $1 billion a year into highways. By 1940, that figure was $2.7 billion, at a time when a billion dollars was real money. The highways government subsidized competed against privately owned, tax-paying railroads and streetcar systems that received no subsidy and were expected to make a profit. What happened? The subsidized way of traveling, by car on government-built highways, drove the unsubsidized railways out of business. No surprise in that.

Today, if you want to go anywhere, you almost always have to drive. Trains are few; flying has become an ordeal, thanks to the Monsters under the Bed Agency – oops, Transportation Security Administration; and the boats that used to connect many of our cities that lie on waterways disappeared along with our trains.

The private automobile is a great way to get around, so long as not very many people have one. Almost every American now has a car, or several cars, which means that we spend more and more time stuck in traffic congestion.

Record gasoline prices, which most experts think will only go higher, make it not only slow and aggravating but also expensive to travel by car. Worse, most of the oil all those cars run on must be imported, much of it from unstable parts of the world. Events beyond our control could easily bring gas crises like those of 1973 and 1979, when you could not buy gas at any price. The gas stations had none to sell.

Our dependence on cars running on imported oil is one of America's greatest national security vulnerabilities. We don't want to find our gas stations empty and us with no way to get around. Nor do we want our kids dying in foreign wars for oil. It is a safe bet we would not have invaded Iraq if that country's main export were bananas.

The best way to reduce our dependence on imported oil is to re-build the network of trains, buses, electric interurban railways and streetcars we had not too many decades ago. We need a National Defense Public Transportation Act, modeled on President Eisenhower's National Defense Interstate Highway Act that built our freeways. The new Act should begin by maintaining the few Amtrak trains and intercity buses we have, along with the public transportation systems in our cities. Then, it would give every county that voted to participate a bus that would connect the county seat with the nearest train. As time went on, it would add more trains, so that a greater portion of the journey was made by train and less by bus (trains are faster and much more comfortable than buses). Gradually, we would put back the public transportation system we used to have, bit by bit. It would again become possible to go from anywhere to anywhere without a car. (Those who would like to learn more about this are welcome to contact Free Congress Foundation for a copy of our study, *A Conservative Proposal for Energy Independence: A National Defense Public Transportation Act.*)

Similarly, we need to bring back the streetcars in our cities. Not only do streetcars contribute to energy independence because they run on electricity, they are also wonderful Retroculture tools for revitalizing decayed urban areas.

Several American cities have already brought the streetcars back, with tremendous positive effects on re-development. Kenosha, Wisconsin, brought streetcars back for just $6.2 million, and the new streetcar line has already generated $150 million in development, for a return on investment of 2,319%. Portland, Oregon, put in a downtown streetcar loop for $55 million; it created over three billion dollars in new development. A 1.2 mile extension of the original loop brought in another $1.35 billion in development.

Why do streetcars bring new development while buses do not? There are several reasons. First, middle-class people with significant disposable income like riding streetcars. They do not like riding buses.

Second, streetcars are "pedestrian facilitators." People who ride through a city on a streetcar tend to get off and on, walking for a while, then riding some more. When they are walking, they go in stores, stop in restaurants for a bite to eat, maybe see a movie or get tickets for a show. In other words, they spend money downtown. Middle-class pedestrians are the life blood of a city, and streetcars make it easy for them to get around.

Third, from a developer's perspective, a streetcar line is a guarantee of high-quality public transportation that will be there for decades. That is not true of buses. A bus line can be here today, gone tomorrow. The investment in track and overhead wire streetcars require mean their routes will not get up and move.

To visualize what Retroculture could do for transportation, imagine that for most of the trips you must now make in your car, including your commute, you could take a streetcar, an interurban (interurbans were big, fast electric streetcars that ran between cities; America had many of them) or a train instead. No worries about gas prices. No worries about traffic congestion, or the weather or the car breaking down. Your household would not need as many cars, which would save you thousands of dollars every year. You just buy a ticket, get on, and relax or read a book while traveling in comfort. Bringing back our trains and streetcars might not be the most important thing the next conservatism has to offer America, but it would certainly be one of the most welcome.

Technology

Some people tell us that new technologies will solve our energy problem and many other problems besides. A few of those promises may come true. History suggests most will not.

One thing the next conservatism must do in the war for Western culture is lead our society to think more deeply than it has about where technology is taking us. Technology has brought some great benefits. But it is also rapidly and radically reshaping our society and our culture in ways conservatives should find troubling.

Genetic engineering is one technology the next conservatism should attempt to stop. We have already noted its importance to Brave New World, where it promises to add genetic conditioning to the psychological conditioning cultural Marxism already uses all too effectively. Genetically engineered crops are already with us; do we want to see genetically engineered children as well? What are the implications of mixing human and animal genes, as is already being done in Britain? Do we not care if our breakfast bacon is partly human? Somehow, the slogan "Just say Yes to cannibalism" is not comforting.

There is another side to genetic engineering few people have considered. Genetic engineering promises new and terrible weapons of war, genetically engineered plagues that could kill tens of millions of people, or destroy crops and cause widespread famine, before cures could be developed. Worse, while nuclear weapons require vast and expensive facilities to build, genetic engineering is knowledge-based. In twenty years, it is something kids may be able to do in the basement. If genetic engineering becomes widespread, honest blunders will create new plagues even without any malign intent.

It may be important to remember that what brought down the Middle Ages was the plague. Contrary to what most Americans are taught, Medieval society was highly successful. It created awe-inspiring structures, in the form of the great cathedrals. It was a prosperous time with rising populations. The Middle Ages developed important new technologies such as the windmill. Most importantly, the Middle Ages represent the closest we ever came to creating a genuinely Christian society. But when the Black Death hit, killing a third, half, sometimes two-thirds of the population in about six weeks, Medieval society dissolved into chaos. What do we think would be the effect of similar death rates on modern society?

The effects of technology are not just a future problem. Cell phones are destroying what little remains of the public space. Who wants to spend time in public places when you are bombarded from all sides with one-half of a private conversation (usually conducted in a loud voice)? At the same time, other technologies such as i-pods allow us to convert public space into private space, sealing ourselves off from the people round us (and their cell phones). The loss of the public realm should trouble conservatives. As in the late Roman Empire, the villas grow more splendid as the fora are abandoned. Is a general retreat into private life a sign that a society is nearing its end?

Most worrisome are the video screen technologies: television, video games (David Grossman has written thoughtfully on how video games condition our kids to kill) and computers tied to the internet. Yes, computers allow us to do some wondrous things. Conservatism has benefited from the internet's bypassing of media gatekeepers, liberals who made sure no conservative voice was heard in the traditional media.

But have we given the downsides sufficient thought? One is a post-literate culture. The generation reared on video games and computers reads little; one wonders if much of it has the attention span to read anything serious. A consequence will be a people cut off from its past. Western culture is mostly a written culture, contained in its great literature, beginning with the Old and New Testaments and the works of the classical Greeks and Romans. When those works go unread, the content of the West's culture runs out into history's sands. If Western culture loses its content, then we lose the war for Western culture, and the West becomes . . . what?

A post-literate people will have little ability to think logically. Reason and logic demand words; images, which are the language of the video screen, feed emotions. Is it any wonder that Americans no longer think but feel? Again, we face a threat to one of the pillars of Western culture. Logic and reason have been particularly Western characteristics. As that pillar crumbles, what will happen to the structure erected upon it, a structure we call the Modern Age?

A people cut off from its past, largely unable to reason and guided primarily by emotion, will be easy to manipulate. In fact, the people will be as easy to manipulate and control as the images on their video screens. We already see this phenomenon all around us, from the power of commercial advertising to the cultural Marxists' use of television as a tool for psychological conditioning. Brave New World relies heavily on manipulation of images to attain the control it desires.

Beyond culture, our questions about the impact of video screen technologies lead to theology, both Jewish and Christian. For 3,000 years, first Judaism and then the Christian church fought a bitter and bloody battle to replace the image with the word. At the heart of Christian faith lies the Word, the Logos: "In the beginning was the Word . . ." What is true for Jerusalem is also true for Athens, the other source of our culture. Through words philosophy rose from the ancient cults and their myths.

But on the video screen, the image is far more powerful than the word. Starting with television, video screens have displaced words with images on a massive scale. The victory the word took 3,000 years to win over the image has been turned to defeat in 30 years. History is running backward. Not surprisingly, paganism is on the rise, beyond and within the church.

So seemingly real have the images become, especially on the computer, that they have spawned a host of virtual realities, in which more and more lost souls live virtual lives. The first Christian principle, and the first principle of Western culture, is that there is and can be only one reality. If there can be more than one reality, we lose both Jerusalem and Athens, the twin sources of our culture. If there can be more than one reality, there can be more than one god; so falls Jerusalem and monotheism. If there can be more than one reality, what is logical in one means nothing in others, where logic itself may not hold; so falls Athens and reason.

As the guardians of Western culture, conservatives should realize that all virtual realities come from Hell. Hell has always hated reality, because in the real world, Christ is King. Now, in the video screen, especially the computer, Hell has found the weapon it has long desired, a mechanism that can create powerful, compelling virtual realities, proliferate them widely, and enable people to live in them much of the time. It has at least a hope of triumphing over reality and making it stick – which comes very close to triumphing over God.

These are weighty matters. Yet for the most part, conservatives have had little to say about them. Some do find the content of many virtual realities disturbing; the Roman arena begins to pale in comparison. But few seem to recognize that the reality principle, that conservative bedrock and Marcuse's old enemy, is itself at stake.

The next conservatism must face this challenge squarely, its eyes open and its thinking cap on. We must evolve a mechanism for evaluating technologies, determining which are acceptable to Western culture and which are inimical to it, and refusing to admit the latter into our lives. This is not a matter for government to decide. As citizens of a republic, we must make such decisions for ourselves, even when that means swimming against the mainstream.

Here, too, we may learn from others. The Amish have long faced the question of what technologies to adopt and which to reject, and they do so in a highly sophisticated manner.

In January of 1999, *Wired* magazine paid a visit to the Amish. They came away highly impressed. Mr. Howard Rheingold, the author of *Virtual Reality* and *The Virtual Community*, who says that "Technology is my native tongue," wrote:

> The Amish communities of Pennsylvania, despite the retro image of horse-drawn buggies and straw

hats, have long been engaged in productive debate about the consequences of technology. . . .

The Amish have an elaborate system by which they evaluate the tools they use; their tentative, at times reluctant use of technology is more complex than a simple rejection or a whole-hearted embrace. What if modern Americans could possibly agree upon criteria for acceptance, as the Amish have? Might we find better ways to wield technological power, other than simply unleashing it and seeing what happens?

The Amish evaluate technologies on the basis of their effects on people and on the kind of life they want to live. One example is the telephone. When telephones first became common, in the early 20th century, the Amish accepted them. But they decided they did not like the results. Conversations over the telephone began to replace people meeting and talking, and the Amish understood that the two are qualitatively different. So they banished the telephone from the house. Amish may have phones, but they have to be in an outbuilding some distance from their home.

Mr. Rheingold wrote,

> I couldn't help thinking it was awfully complicated to have a phone you used only for calling back – from a booth in a meadow. Why not make life easier and just put one in the house?

"What would that lead to?" another Amish man asked me. "We don't want to be the kind of people who will interrupt a conversation at home to answer a telephone. It's not just how you use the technology that concerns us. We're also concerned about what kind of person you become when you use it."

Similarly, the Amish can use electricity, but not from the grid. They have to generate it themselves. When Mr. Rheingold asked one Amish man why, he replied,

> "The Bible teaches us not to conform to the world, to keep a separation. Connecting to the electric lines would make too many things too easy. Pretty soon people would start plugging in radios and televisions, and that's like a hot line to the modern world."

The Amish also use diesel engines, but even if a piece of farm equipment has an engine to run part of the machinery, it must still be horse-drawn. Why?

> The bishops don't want increased efficiency to interfere with the practice of fathers and sons, mothers and daughters, working together with horse-drawn machinery and hand-held implements. . . . "Does it bring us together, or draw us apart?" is the primary question the bishops ask in considering whether to permit or put away a technology. . . .
> "The Amish employ an intuitive sense about what will build solidarity and what will pull them apart," says Donald Kraybill, author of *The Riddle of Amish Culture*. "You find state-of-the-art barbeques on some Amish porches. Here is a tool they see as increasing family coherence: Barbeques bring people together."

Mr. Rheingold concludes that "Far from knee-jerk techno-phobes, these [the Amish] are very adaptive techno-selectives who devise remarkable technologies that fit within their self-imposed limits." We think that well describes the approach the next conservatism needs to take toward technology. Unlike the Amish, whose bishops decide which technologies to accept, which to adapt and which to reject, conservatives will have to make those decisions for themselves.

The Amish have succeeded in maintaining their traditional, conservative, Christian culture in a hostile modern world because they have, to some extent, separated themselves from the surrounding society. That separation is not complete. The Amish vote and pay taxes. They go to doctors and hospitals. They help their "English" neighbors as well as other Amish. But the Amish are sufficiently separate that they do not drown in the flood of sewage that is American pop culture.

Secession

Here again we come to a question, not merely of tactics, but of strategy. In our view, the next conservatism should call on conservatives to separate themselves to some extent from those elements in our society which promote decadence. Retroculture inherently calls for such separation. If we intend to recapture past ways of thinking, acting and living, then we will automatically separate ourselves from those who continue following the latest fashions.

In 1999, Paul Weyrich wrote a now-famous open letter to the conservative movement. In that letter, he suggested that instead of trying to retake existing institutions from the cultural Marxists, a battle conservatives are unlikely to win, we separate our lives and the lives of our families from those institutions and build new institutions for ourselves, institutions that reflect our beliefs.

In that letter, he wrote,

What I mean by separation is, for example, what the

homeschoolers have done. Faced with public school systems that no longer educate but instead "condition" students with the attitudes demanded by Political Correctness, they have seceded. They have separated themselves from public schools and created new institutions, new schools, in their homes.

This form of separation, in which as conservatives we would build our own institutions, is what political scientists call "creating parallel structures." It is a profoundly revolutionary act, far more so than carrying banners saying "World Revolution Now." But when the power structures are virtually all in the hands of the cultural Marxists and in service to Brave New World, is not the cultural restoration we seek a revolutionary act? We hasten to add, lest we be quoted out of context, that this revolution is entirely peaceful.

The next conservatism's strategic goal, to be attained by creating parallel structures, should not be permanent separation from the rest of society. Rather, it should be to re-take the whole of our society for our traditional culture, by the power of example. But what examples can we offer if our lives are trapped in institutions controlled by our culture's enemies? If we are to duplicate the success of the cultural Marxists' "long march through the institutions," to use Gramsci's phrase, we must begin by creating institutions where our beliefs can manifest themselves in good works others can see.

When Mr. Weyrich wrote his open letter, some people misinterpreted what he said as a call for conservatives to abandon politics. He said no such thing. Conservatives must remain politically active, to prevent the cultural Marxists from mobilizing all the power of the state to crush us and forbid the expression of our beliefs (as has already happened on more than one university campus). What he did say is that we cannot reasonably expect to win the war for Western culture through politics alone, because culture is stronger than politics. Conservatives must continue our work in politics, but we must also do something more, something that works directly on the culture.

That "something," we have suggested, is Retroculture. In this chapter, we have illustrated a variety of ways in which we can fight the culture war by recovering old ways of thinking and of living. There are undoubtedly countless more. Many will require us to separate ourselves from the decadent cultural mainstream and build our own institutions. Again, there are many more ways to do that than we have discussed here. One young correspondent, a Retroculture enthusiast, suggested establishing Retroculture Centers all across the country where like-minded people could gather and combine their efforts.

Everything we have suggested is compatible with the next conservatism's other goal of restoring the republic, because Retroculture demands little of government other than it get out of our way. You can be certain it will not do that willingly, which is another reason why conservatives must remain in politics. Restoring the republic, too, is a revolutionary act, a revolution that can only be carried out through politics. Politics is necessary to the next conservatism, but not sufficient. The next conservatism calls on us to do more, not less.

Dare we yet hope, so late in the day, to win the war for Western culture? Retroculture says we can. What worked in the past can work again. We *can* go back.

Chapter Four

Governing America: National Security

So far, we have discussed the next conservatism's two principal goals, restoring the republic and winning the war for Western culture. In the next three chapters, we will consider means: how conservatives ought to govern America, should we ever again get the chance.

The next conservatism's governance would be dramatically different from what we have seen from supposedly conservative presidents and Congresses in recent years. Why? Because it would govern within the limitations imposed by a restored republic. Put simply, that means there are many things government, especially the federal government, ought not do. Even things that might seem good in themselves – bringing peace and order to foreign lands, teaching American schoolchildren to read, encouraging us to conserve water – are not good when the federal government engages in them. A restored American republic will not wage "wars of choice" to bring "freedom" to peoples who do not know what the word means. It will not force rote memorization on schoolchildren so they pass some government-mandated test, for fear some child be "left behind." (Like Greeks bearing gifts, beware of governments prating about "children": it is always a trick.) It will not tell us we must install "low flow" shower heads and water closets in our homes. Can anyone imagine King

George III dictating to the American colonists the sorts of chamber pots they must use?

What are the legitimate roles of a republican government? The history of the American republic suggests there are two: ensuring national security and providing infrastructure – navigable waterways, railways, roads, etc. – without which trade is not possible

Looking back even further, to the rise of the state in the 15th and 16th centuries, we find states originally had just one role: maintaining order. As Martin van Creveld argues in *The Rise and Decline of the State*, the state was born to bring order, nothing more. It did that successfully, which gave the state legitimacy. The state's present crisis of legitimacy arises in part from the fact that it no longer maintains order, as attested by high crime rates, the explosion of private security services and the rise of "gated communities," which is the new name for castles.

Here, drawing on American precedent, we will broaden the legitimate functions of a republican government beyond order to security, of which order remains the most important component. (Providing infrastructure remains a legitimate function as well.) In the next three chapters, we will consider three separable but interconnected aspects of security: national security, economic security and moral security. We begin with national security, which means something quite different for a restored American republic than it does for an all-intrusive national security state.

Local Police

For the next conservatism, national security starts not with a behemoth Pentagon or an Orwellian Department of Homeland Security but with local police. The most important aspect of national security is security where we live. Not only does the state – any state, republic or not – owe us a life free from crime, it owes us a life free from fear of crime. If we must worry constantly about the safety of our person, family and property, living behind barred windows and doors, putting alarms on our houses and cars, fearful of letting our children play outside without adult supervision, the state has failed in its most basic responsibility. It has failed to provide order.

Local order depends on local police. The job of local police is not responding to crime, but preventing crime before it happens. Response comes too late; civic order has already been disrupted.

Here as elsewhere, tradition shows us what works. What works is the neighborhood cop. He walks or cycles a regular beat in the same neighborhood, day in and day out, year in and year out. He knows the people who live there and they know him. He knows what is normal and what is out of place in his neighborhood. He talks to people, and they tell him what is going on. He protects his neighborhood, and the neighborhood protects him. That is how the famous British "Bobby" worked, and it was why he did not need to carry a gun.

In modern parlance, this is called "community policing." Expanding community policing is an important part of the next conservatism's agenda. It is national security writ small, as conservatives would write it, consistent with our desire to "Think locally, act locally."

Our policy should be for every neighborhood in America to have its cop on the beat. Under a republic's principle of subsidiarity, providing community policing is mostly a function of local government. But if we are to reach our goal, the federal government may need to provide the local level some resources. Community policing is expensive. It requires a lot of police. It is more efficient to put cops in cruisers and have them respond to calls. Unfortunately, that is also far less effective in preventing crime.

Until recently, there was a wonderful program to provide community police called the Police Corps. It was a police ROTC. It offered college scholarships in return for a four-year commitment to serve as a community policeman after graduation. The Police Corps did its own training, which the authors of this book were privileged to witness, and its training was far more thorough than that at most police academies. The program was established in more than thirty states.

What happened to the Police Corps? With some help from Congress, the Bush administration killed it. A White House spokesman said, "We think money is better spent on the Department of Homeland Security than on local police." Once again, we see how "conservatism" was distorted by Washington in recent years. No real conservative would ever fall for that line.

The next conservatism should revive and expand the Police Corps, as a good way to provide the large number of policemen community policing requires. It also offers college scholarships for the type of young person who wants to be a cop, which will benefit society the same way the GI bill did. It will help young people join the middle class.

It may be that local communities will need more support than one program can provide if they are to create effective community policing. If so, the federal government should provide that support. Far better we should spend some millions of federal dollars securing our homes and neighborhoods than throw away trillions trying to secure countries on the other side of the earth. Real national security begins – literally – at home.

A Different Kind of National Security

This perspective, that a successful national security policy leaves us safer in our homes and neighborhoods, should shape the next conservatism's thinking about national security writ large as well as writ small. If what America does in the world motivates others to attack us at home, then we should probably be doing something else. Republics mind their own business. They do not, in John Quincy Adams's words, go abroad in search of monsters to destroy. When Washington uses stealth bombers and cruise missiles to destroy other peoples' homes in the name of "democracy," those "hi-tech" weapons turn into boomerangs.

The next conservatism recognizes that America needs a different grand strategy. A grand strategy is a country's overarching idea about how it intends to relate to the rest of the world. Foreign policy and defense policy flow from grand strategy (at least they should), and must be consistent with it.

Currently, America is following an offensive grand strategy. We are trying to press "democratic capitalism" (really Brave New World) on the rest of the globe, by force of arms if necessary. This was as true under President Bill Clinton as under George W. Bush; just ask the Serbs, a Christian people the Clinton administration bombed for almost three months to compel them to yield their ancestral homeland, Kosovo, to Moslems. Not only did an offensive grand strategy lead us to folly in the Balkans and into a morass in Iraq, it has undermined our moral standing almost everywhere. As Russell Kirk wrote, the surest way to make someone your enemy is to tell him you are going to remake him in your image for his own good.

Through most of our history, America followed a defensive grand strategy. We did not seek to dictate to or rule over others. We avoided playing the power games typical of Great Powers, games that usually lead to war. We related actively to the rest of the world, but we did so through private means, trade and ideas, not through government. Following a defensive grand strategy, we avoided Europe's conflicts, expanded our trade and economy, kept the federal government small, preserved our liberties and became a "shining city on a hill," a moral example that inspired people everywhere. Our forefathers knew that the power of example is not only the safest but also the most potent form of power.

The next conservatism calls on our country to return to the defensive grand strategy that served it so well. Some critics will say, "You can't win if you stay on the defensive." The great 19th century German military theorist Carl von Clausewitz would disagree. He believed that the defensive was the stronger form of war. Early in his book *On War*, which is rightly considered a classic, Clausewitz writes,

> Defense is simply the stronger form of war, the one that makes the enemy's defeat more certain. . . . We maintain unequivocally that the form of warfare that we call defense not only offers greater probability of victory than attack, but that its victories can attain the same proportions and results.

In his 2004 re-election campaign, President George W. Bush said over and over that America must remain on the offensive. To cite just one example, he told an audience in Philadelphia, "No question, we will win the war on terror by staying on the offensive. This administration and this leadership is committed to making sure we stay on the offensive against the terrorists."

In contrast, here is Clausewitz again:

So in order to state the relationship precisely, we must say that the defensive form of warfare is intrinsically stronger than the offensive. This is the point that we have been trying to make, for although it is implicit in the nature of the matter and experience has confirmed it again and again, it is at odds with prevalent opinion, which proves how ideas can be confused by superficial writers.

And, it seems, by superficial presidents.

What might a defensive grand strategy for America look like in the 21st century? It will be different from what it was in the 19th century, because conditions are different. As we noted in our chapter on restoring the republic, all over the world states are suffering a crisis of legitimacy. People are transferring their first loyalty away from the state to many other things: races, religions, ideologies, "causes," business enterprises, gangs, etc. The next conservatism's defensive grand strategy will have to work in a world where the state is in decline.

One consequence of this decline is a rise in what Washington calls "terrorism." President George W. Bush called on Americans to fight an (endless) "war on terrorism." This is misleading. The threat America and other states face is not merely terrorism, which is only a technique. The threat is Fourth Generation warfare, which is a vastly broader phenomenon. (We will consider the other three generations in our discussion of military reform.) It is the biggest change in warfare since the Peace of Westphalia that ended the Thirty Years War in 1648. Westphalia gave the state a monopoly on war. The Fourth Generation takes that monopoly away. All over the world, states are fighting non-state opponents such as al Qaeda, Hezbollah and MS-13. Almost everywhere, the state is losing.

Fourth Generation war is likely to dominate the 21st century. It is important that conservatives, most of whom are concerned with national security, understand it thoroughly. It has three central characteristics:

* The loss of the state's monopoly on war and the rise of non-state entities for which more and more people are willing to fight. These entities, again, include gangs, religions, races and ethnic groups within races, regions, tribes, business enterprises, "causes" such as animal rights – the variety is almost limitless;
* A return to a world of cultures, not just states, in conflict. Other cultures will not fight the way the West does, with formal armies, navies and air forces. Much of what we call "terrorism" is traditional Arab light cavalry warfare, carried out on a world scale with new technologies; and
* The decline of the state and the rise of alternative, often cultural, primary loyalties not only "over there," but here, in America itself.

Colonel John Boyd, USAF, America's greatest military theorist, defined grand strategy as the art of connecting yourself to as many independent power centers as possible while isolating the enemy from as many independent power centers as possible. What does Colonel Boyd's definition of grand strategy mean in a world dominated by the decline of the state and the rise of Fourth Generation war?

It means we should seek to connect our country with as many centers and sources of order as possible while isolating America from as many centers and sources of disorder as possible. The great division in our 21st-century world will not be between "democracies" and countries that are "not free." It will be between places that are ordered and places that are disordered. Conservatism's first principle is the need for order. That principle will have to become the basis of America's grand strategy in an increasingly disordered world.

What do we mean by centers and sources of order? Mostly, places where the state still stands. While the crisis of legitimacy of the state is universal, that does not mean it will everywhere reach catastrophic proportions. Those places where the state endures will remain centers of (relative) order. America is already connected to those places in a variety of ways and should remain so.

In turn, one of the primary centers of disorder in the 21st century will be failed states, areas where the state has disappeared, or become simply one criminal gang among many. Examples include much of Africa, Somalia, Mesopotamia (since the American invasion destroyed the Iraqi state), parts of the former Soviet Union and the West Bank of the Jordan River. These areas represent the future for much of the world.

Cultures, too, tend toward order or disorder. In traditional, Confucian Chinese culture, order is the highest virtue. A Confucian China could be one of the world's most influential centers and sources of order.

Another culture shows that centers of disorder and sources of disorder may not be identical: Islam. Because Islam is a religion of rules, it is capable of providing internal order to Islamic societies. But Islam is likely to be one of the main sources of disorder in the 21st century, because Islam demands its believers wage endless *jihad* in the non-Islamic world.

One way in which centers of disorder will act as sources of disorder will be by producing hordes of refugees and immigrants. It is natural to flee disorder. But as some European countries have already discovered to their cost, accepting refugees from centers of disorder imports disorder. Just as people from highly ordered cultures, such as Germans and Scandinavians, take order with them wherever they go, so people from disordered cultures are bearers of chaos. Air-tight border controls and a hard-nosed immigration policy will be critically important in isolating America from world disorder.

This brings us to the next element of our proposed grand strategy: what do we mean by "connect" and "isolate"? Connection is easy enough to understand. Goods, money, people and ideas all flow freely with minimal barriers. Americans view those to whom we are connected as friends, extending help in times of need and also receiving their assistance. Commercially, we buy their products and they reciprocate by buying ours.

"Isolate" is more difficult to understand, in part because the Globalists present "isolationism" as a bogeyman. September 11, 2001, should have taught us that in a Fourth Generation world, our physical security will depend on our ability and willingness to isolate ourselves from hostile forces.

In general, isolation will mean minimizing flows of people, money, materials and ideas, especially ideas that represent new primary loyalties such as alien religions and ideologies, into the United States. In some situations, isolation will require actions that may appear harsh by current standards (which have often been set by cultural Marxists). We may find it necessary to prohibit people from certain places from entering the U.S. We may need to profile on a variety of bases, including religious belief and ethnic origin. Isolation may also inflict hardships on Americans, as when we must avoid becoming dependent on imports from disordered areas. Oil from the Middle East and West Africa is an example.

How does this grand strategy of connection and isolation work to isolate our enemy, which means centers and sources of disorder, from other independent power centers? Here, the next conservatism's grand strategy works indirectly, in a way Colonel Boyd might appreciate. To use one of his favorite expressions, it folds the enemy back on himself.

As the offensive grand strategy of the Bush administration has demonstrated, when we choose to attack centers and sources of disorder, we provide an external threat against which our enemies can unite. Conversely, if we isolate ourselves from them, we will help them focus on and accentuate their internal contradictions. This is a classic case of inaction being a form of action.

The Islamic world offers an example. Islam mandates *jihad* against all non-Islamics, which means Islam will always be a threat to some degree. But Islam is also riven with internal conflicts. Were America to isolate herself from the Islamic world, we would help focus Islamic energies inward. We would fold Islam back on itself.

Here we see clearly why America's grand strategy should be defensive. When we tell Moslems that we intend to remake them in our image – as Michael Scheuer put it, to allow Mrs. Mohammed to vote, vamp and abort – they have little choice but to fight us. In contrast, a defensive grand strategy leaves Islamic societies alone, to be whatever they want to be. They have less reason to focus on us, leaving them to fight among themselves.

The logic of a defensive grand strategy is almost self-evident. If our goal is to connect ourselves to order, we will not want to go on the offensive against other states, which are centers of order. If successful, such offensives are likely to destroy the opposing state and reduce it to another center of stateless disorder, as happened in Iraq. In turn, offensives against centers and sources of disorder run contrary to our desire to isolate ourselves from disorder. As we see in Afghanistan and in Iraq, the surest way to enmesh ourselves in a center of disorder is to invade and occupy it. Sadly, we are likely to import disorder from both places back into the United States.

Don't Kick Sand in Our Face

A defensive grand strategy does not mean we allow ourselves to be kicked around. Here again, Clausewitz is helpful:

> What is the concept of defense? The parrying of a blow. What is its characteristic feature? Awaiting the blow. It is this feature that turns any action into a defensive one; it is the only test by which defense can be distinguished from attack in war. Pure defense, however, would be completely contrary to the idea of war, since it would mean that only one side was waging it. Therefore, defense in war can only be relative, and the characteristic feature of waiting should be applied only to the basic concept, not to all of its components.

In simple terms, this means that we would leave centers and sources of disorder alone, militarily and in other ways, unless they attacked us. But if they attacked us, our response would be Roman, which is to say annihilating.

In some cases, delivering an annihilating response may require us to use unconventional weapons. When that is the case, it will be imperative that our counterattack follow instantly after an attack on the United States. It must appear to be a "spasm" on our part, not a calculated act. In 1914, had Austria-Hungary declared war on Serbia within 48 hours of the assassination of the Archduke Franz Ferdinand, she would probably have gotten away with it without starting a general European war. Similarly, had we responded to 9/11 in 48 hours with an attack on Afghanistan that wiped al Qaeda-held areas off the map, the world might have accepted it. Certainly, we would not be bogged down in a guerilla war in Afghanistan six years later.

A defensive grand strategy that includes an annihilating military counterattack is consistent with our goal of isolating America from centers and sources of disorder while folding them back on themselves, yet it runs no danger of being perceived as weakness on our part. On the contrary, it both demonstrates and demands more strength of will than is currently evident in Washington, in either political party.

One theme shines through this description of a defensive grand strategy: the requirement that America not let itself be dependent on any part of the world that is a center or source of disorder. Here, the main implication is for our country's economic policy. While the United States need not pursue a policy of autarky, it does require what might best be termed full economic independence. That is to say, we need to be able to manage on what we've got if we have to, in terms both of natural resources and manufacturing capability. Obviously, this goes directly against the demands of the Globalists.

A Different Foreign Policy

A defensive grand strategy, which is a major change from our current offensive grand strategy, logically leads to a different foreign policy. In 1951, one of America's true conservatives, Senator Robert A. Taft, published a book titled *A Foreign Policy for Americans*. What he recommended then is what the next conservatism should stand for now. In discussing the purposes of American foreign policy, Senator Taft wrote:

There are a good many Americans who talk about an American century in which America will dominate the world. They rightly point out that the United States is so powerful today that we should assume a moral leadership in the world. . . . The trouble with those who advocate this policy is that they really do not confine themselves to moral leadership. . . . In their hearts they want to force on these foreign peoples through use of American money, and even, perhaps, American arms, the policies which moral leadership is able to advance only through the sound strength of its principles and the force of its persuasion. I do not think this moral leadership ideal justifies our engaging in any preventive war. . . . I do not believe any policy which has behind it the threat of military force is justified as part of the basic foreign policy of the United States except to defend the liberty of our own people.

Like the Founding Fathers, Senator Taft valued liberty at home above "superpower" status abroad. The next conservatism looks at foreign policy from the same perspective. Do we now have a foreign policy that requires a federal government, particularly an Executive branch, so powerful that it is a danger to our liberties? If we do, then we have a fundamental contradiction at the heart of our foreign policy. Why? Because the first purpose of our foreign policy should be to preserve our liberties.

As Senator Taft understood, this touches on the most sensitive foreign policy question: to what degree should America be active in the world? Since his time, the whole Washington Establishment has come to condemn his position, which is the real conservative position, as "isolationism." But the word itself is a lie. America was never isolated from the rest of the world. Rather, through most of our history America related actively to the rest of the world, but it did so through private means, through trade and by serving as a moral example to the world, the "shining city on a hill." That policy preserved our liberties while making us, as Senator Taft wrote, "respected as the most disinterested and charitable nation in the world."

Then, after World War II, we began to play the Great Power game the Founding Fathers warned us against. Because of the threat of Communism, that was necessary for a time. But when Communism fell in the early 1990s, we did not return to our historic foreign policy. Instead, the Washington Establishment declared America the dominant power in the world, "the only superpower," the New Rome as some would have it. We set off on the course of American empire, despite the fact that empire abroad almost certainly means the eventual extinction of liberty here at home.

The next conservatism needs a different foreign policy, a foreign policy designed for a republic, not an empire. The Establishment wants to play the Great Power game because it lives richly off that game. But the next conservatism is about throwing the Establishment out, not enriching it further. The next conservatism's foreign policy should proceed from these wise words of Senator Robert A. Taft:

> I do not believe it is a selfish goal for us to insist that the overriding purpose of all American foreign policy should be the maintenance of the liberty and peace of our people in the United States, so that they may achieve that intellectual and material improvement which is their genius and in which they can set an example for all peoples. By that example we can do an even greater service to mankind than we can do by billions of material assistance – and more than we can ever do by war.

Patriotism v. Nationalism

Some people who say they are conservatives may react to this call for prudence and modesty in American foreign policy by labeling its advocates "unpatriotic." Nothing could be further from the truth. In fact, those who demand America grasp for world dominion are not patriots themselves, but nationalists.

From its outset more than 200 years ago, conservative thought has drawn a sharp distinction between patriotism and nationalism. Patriotism is attachment to the local, the real, the concrete: to one's own place, one's own farm or town or valley and its traditions. Nationalism, in contrast, is abstract, a fanatical devotion to the idea of a country: the Fatherland, the Motherland, *la Patrie*. While patriotism looks locally, nationalism grasps globally.

Nationalism originated not on the political right but on the left, in the 18th century. It was one of the many horrors unleashed on the world by the French Revolution. In *The Rise and Decline of the State*, Martin van Creveld writes,

> Even as the state was reaching maturity around the middle of the eighteenth century, however, forces were at work which were about to transform it from an instrument [to bring order] into an end and, later, a living god. . . .
> The man who did more than anyone else to start the Great Transformation was, perhaps, Jean-Jacques Rousseau. . . . It was only in the years after 1789 [the year of the French Revolution], when some of the intellectuals came to power and when their ruminations were married to the pretensions of the state, that . . . nationalism took on an aggressive, bellicose character.

Regrettably, both in America and in other countries

nationalism has retained its aggressive, bellicose character. Too often, that has led to war. In 1914, nationalism led the European peoples to welcome an unnecessary war that would prove disastrous for Western civilization. World War I gave us Lenin, Hitler, and ultimately Europe's loss of faith in itself. As van Creveld writes,

> Reveling in total war, the state demanded and obtained sacrifice on a scale which, had they been able to imagine it, would have made even the old Aztec gods blanch.

America's entry into World War I was engineered by President Woodrow Wilson, who won re-election in 1916 on the slogan, "He kept us out of war." Within a month of his inauguration in 1917, he demanded from Congress a declaration of war on Germany. Wilson was a liberal, or "Progressive" as liberals were then called. The Progressives knew the only way they could overturn our republican traditions and create the vast, powerful federal government they desired was by going to war. In wartime, any expansion of government can be sold on the basis that "we must do it to win the war." Wilson and the Progressives got what they wanted, war and Leviathan.

Contrary to the left's attempts to label conservatives "warmongers," true conservatives have always feared and hated war. No force is more powerful in overturning traditions and forcing radical social and cultural change. Communism could never have taken over Russia except as a consequence of World War I. Feminism's victory in drawing women away from home and family and into traditionally male careers owes much to women's move into the labor force in both World Wars. The same labor shortage drew millions of American Negroes away from the rural south into northern urban ghettoes, where families weakened and rural traditions withered. It is radicals and revolutionaries, not conservatives, whose goals are furthered by war.

Patriotism, in contrast to nationalism, offers no road to war, because its attachment is local. In his *Reflections on the Revolution in France*, Edmund Burke, modern conservatism's founder, drew this essential distinction between patriotism and nationalism:

> It is boasted . . . that all local ideas should be sunk, and that the people should no longer be Gascons, Picards, Bretons, Normans; but Frenchmen, with one country, one heart, and one Assembly. . . . No man was ever attached by a sense of pride, partiality or real affection, to a description of square measurement. . . . We begin our public affections in our families. We pass on to our neighborhoods, and our habitual provincial connections . . .

The next conservatism's slogan of "Think locally, act locally" is not new to conservative thought. We find it in Burke, and the writings of many conservatives since Burke. Voltaire was no conservative, but the next conservatism happily takes one bit of advice he offered: it prefers to see America cultivate her own garden.

Military Reform

Of course, the next conservatism recognizes that in the world as it is, America must be able to defend herself. Conservatives have always stood for a strong national defense. As Trotsky said, you may not be interested in war, but war is interested in you. War can be forced on America by the actions of others, and we must be prepared.

However, here too the next conservatism moves beyond past conservative agendas. During the Cold War, most conservatives defined a strong national defense as simply giving the Pentagon more money. The next conservatism looks beyond the size of the Pentagon's budget – which now equals what all the other countries in the world together spend for defense – to consider how wisely the money is spent. We cannot buy national security like chopped liver, by the pound. If our military buys the wrong weapons and employs outdated tactics, it will lose regardless of how much money we spend. France's Maginot Line cost a great deal more than Germany's Panzer divisions, but in 1940, the Panzers simply went around the Maginot Line, and France fell.

The next conservatism recognizes that the Pentagon is a bureaucracy, and it behaves no differently from any other government bureaucracy. Its focus is less winning wars than acquiring and justifying more resources, expanding its bureaucratic empire and creating career opportunities for senior officers. Conservatives should be no less skeptical of military bureaucrats than of any other bureaucrats.

For this reason, the next conservatism embraces military reform. In the 1970s and 1980s, some conservatives and liberals on Capitol Hill, most prominently Congressman Newt Gingrich and Senator Gary Hart, joined with younger military officers and some outside defense thinkers (including Colonel John Boyd) to create the military reform movement. Bill Lind was one of those thinkers, and Paul Weyrich strongly supported the military reform movement. Its goal was to ask of every defense program, "Does this make sense in terms of winning in combat?" Too often, it found that the answer was "no" for programs the Pentagon wanted, while real and pressing defense needs were being overlooked.

Some of the major themes of the military reform movement included:

* Putting people and ideas before hardware.
* Buying simpler weapons that work in the complexity and chaos of combat and that are affordable in adequate numbers.
* Adopting tactics based on speed, surprise and maneuver rather than firepower and attrition.
* Subjecting new weapons to realistic tests that mimic actual combat, and refusing to buy those that fail.
* Promoting people who show the boldness, imagination and strength of character to lead successfully in war instead of bureaucrats and office politicians.
* Reducing the size of the bloated senior officer corps so junior leaders have opportunities to make decisions.

The military reform movement died as a political force in the late 1980s, overwhelmed by the vast amount of money the Pentagon and the defense industry could give Senators and Congressman and their states and districts. It is hard to fight money with ideas.

Four Generations of Warfare

But the military reformers continued to develop their ideas. In the late 1980s, Bill Lind came up with an intellectual framework called the "Four Generations of Modern War" that has garnered extensive interest world-wide (except, of course, in the Pentagon). It suggests that the U.S. military is dangerously behind the power curve in terms of where war is going – not just one generation behind, but two.

The First Generation began with the Peace of

Westphalia in 1648 and ran to about the time of the American Civil War. In general, battlefields during those two centuries were orderly, with line-and-column tactics. The battlefield of order produced a military culture of order, which still characterizes state militaries.

Around the middle of the 19th century, the order of the battlefield began to break down. Combat became more and more disorderly. That created the central problem still facing state armed services: the military culture of order became increasingly contradictory to the nature of the battlefield. In effect, state militaries found themselves with one foot on the dock and one foot on a moving boat.

Second and Third Generation war were two different attempts to resolve this contradiction. The Second Generation, which was developed by the French army during and after World War I, attempted to reimpose order on the battlefield through centrally controlled application of massive firepower (it is sometimes called firepower/attrition warfare). The Second Generation maintained and reinforced the First Generation culture of order. It focused inward, on rules, orders, processes and methods; it remained highly centralized, with almost all decisions made at the top of the hierarchy; it wanted obedience, not initiative; and it depended on top-down, imposed discipline.

Stuck in Second Generation Warfare

The U.S. military learned Second Generation war from the French, and it remains the American way of war today, with the partial exception of the U.S. Marine Corps. The U.S. military fights by putting firepower on targets. It does that very well, possibly better than anyone else in the world. But that is all it can do, and there is a bit more to war than that.

Third Generation war, also called maneuver warfare,

was developed by the German army in World War I, not World War II, although most people know it as Blitzkrieg. Instead of just putting firepower on targets, it used speed, surprise and maneuvers deep into the enemy's rear area to shatter enemy units and leave them unable to function. To make these tactics possible, the German army broke with the First Generation culture of order. It focused outward on the situation, the enemy, and the result the situation required; it de-centralized decision-making radically, using orders that told the subordinate what result to get but leaving up to him how to do it; it prized initiative over obedience; and it depended on self-discipline.

In 1940, the Second Generation French army and Third Generation German army met in combat. By almost every measure, the French, with their British, Dutch and Belgian allies, were stronger than the Germans. The allies had more tanks than the Germans and better tanks. But Germany won in just six weeks, using maneuver warfare.

While the U.S. military has remained stuck in the Second Generation, war is moving on into the Fourth. We are two generations behind. We have already discussed Fourth Generation war, and we will not repeat that discussion here. But it is important to understand that against Fourth Generation opponents, Second Generation war is useless. Why? Fourth Generation fighters wear no uniforms, have no tanks or fighter planes, and blend into the civilian population. Second Generation war puts firepower on targets, but Fourth Generation fighters are untargetable. The Second and Fourth Generations are ships passing in the night. That is why the world's most richly resourced, best trained, "hi-tech" military, our own, has been fought to a standstill in Iraq and Afghanistan by Fourth Generation opponents whose budgets, if graphed on the same scale as our own, would not be visible.

The next conservatism's defense policy should have as its top priority moving the U.S. armed forces out of the Second Generation and into the Third, as a necessary (though not itself sufficient) step to facing Fourth Generation war. This means reviving military reform. Most of the recommendations of the old Military Reform Movement remain valid, and will help move us into the Third Generation. The most important reform is reform of the American armed services' institutional cultures, to make them outward-focused and de-centralized, prizing initiative over obedience and depending on self-discipline. As most soldiers, sailors, Marines and airmen will tell you, that will be an enormous, and difficult, change.

There is a bit of icing on this cake: moving beyond the Second Generation should allow defense spending to fall at the same time that our ability to win in combat increases. Most of the "big ticket" weapons programs the Pentagon wants are Second Generation "legacy" systems, useful only for fighting other Second Generation state militaries. As military reformers like to say, what is the Air Force's vaunted, "stealth" F-22 fighter useful for? To shoot down Taliban flying carpets.

There is one other area where the next conservatism needs to take on the Pentagon bureaucracy: missile defense. Conservatives have long been proponents of missile defense, and rightly so. Just one intercontinental ballistic missile, with a nuclear warhead, launched intentionally by a "rogue state" or by accident by China or Russia, could wipe out a major American city. We could have a million people dead, not the 3,000 of 9/11.

It is more probable that a nuclear weapon will be smuggled into America in a shipping container by a Fourth Generation enemy such as al Qaeda. Once again we see that in the face of Fourth Generation war, nothing is more important than effective control of our borders.

But the missile threat is still real enough that it is folly not to protect ourselves from it. The problem is, in typical bureaucratic fashion, the Pentagon has spent more than $100 billion on missile defense, and we have almost nothing to show for the money.

We need to take missile defense out of the hands of the Pentagon bureaucrats who have done nothing and create a special program, run by a few people who can be held accountable, that can go in a different direction. There are several promising possibilities. One is the space-based missile defense President Reagan favored. Another is modifying the Aegis anti-aircraft system on some Navy ships to give it an anti-missile capability. We need to make this a top priority. The next conservatism says that national security means the security of our families and communities. Nothing threatens that security more direly than the prospect of a nuclear attack.

Homeland Security

This brings us back where we started, to homeland security. What the next conservatism seeks to secure is our hearths and homes, our farms and firesides, not "democracy" in Karjackistan.

It is no coincidence that when America eschewed empire and followed a defensive grand strategy, our homeland seldom faced much of a threat. We did not need to be "security conscious," which is to say fearful. When it was time to board an airplane, we just walked out an airport door and got on. Once America returns to a defensive grand strategy, the need for "homeland security" should diminish. That is genuine homeland security: not constantly being prepared against an attack, but not needing to fear an attack.

There will, of course, always be some level of danger. But a republic is not a nursery. Its answer to danger is courage and an active citizenry, not a "nanny state" that promises to keep us safe if we surrender our liberties. That is the road to Brave New World.

Here again, the next conservatism's motto, "Think locally, act locally" applies. Whether danger comes from fire or flood, crime or terrorism, it should be met first on the local level. Citizens should be encouraged to act, not told to wait for "professionals" to deal with the problem. The passengers on United 93 on 9/11, who organized themselves to retake their aircraft from the terrorists and thereby prevented a possible attack on the White House, should be our model. If legislation is needed to protect citizens who act in an emergency from lawsuits or other legal liability, conservatives should ensure such legislation gets passed.

The next line of defense is local police, especially community police. The only way to defeat terrorist attacks, like ordinary crimes, is by preventing them. Once one has taken place, even "first response" is too late. Our security has been shattered. Cops who know their beats and can sense where and when something is wrong are our most important defenders.

If we need another line of defense, the next conservatism should consider reviving an old American tradition: the militia. Because a militia is organized from individual communities, it too, like neighborhood cops, knows what is going on. Also like local police, a militia does not serve Leviathan, a federal government that seeks to snoop endlessly in ordinary citizens' lives. This militia would be organized by individual states, as they saw a need for it. (It would not be a private militia, which can be dangerous in a world of Fourth Generation war.) It might report to county sheriffs, local, elected officials who posses substantial common law powers. Under no circumstances should it be controlled by or report to Washington.

The next conservatism should seek to abolish the Department of Homeland Security. The arguments against it are strong. It answers only to Big Brother. It has already become Pentagon II, absorbing vast resources while producing very little. Its necessary functions can be performed by traditional agencies such as the FBI.

It is simply not possible for something like the Department of Homeland Security not to endanger our liberties. All its incentives work the other way. Like all other federal bureaucracies, DHS will seek more power, more money, more bureaucratic empire. Against those powerful inbred drives, what is to keep it from tearing up the Bill of Rights? Mere rhetoric – and the dubious protection offered by our courts.

From the perspective of the federal government, fear is a growth industry. The more the public can be made fearful, the greater federal police powers can grow. If the bulk of police power is local, not federal, Americans will not confront Leviathan when they face a law enforcement officer. It is far easier to approach the town mayor or council with an issue of abuse of police powers than it is to confront a faceless federal bureaucracy. If we cast our liberties before anyone who promises to "protect us," like pearls before swine, we will find in short order that we are neither safe nor free.

Immigration

Most of the issues addressed in the chapter are long-term.

105

It takes time to turn the ship of state. But there is one issue that will not wait. That issue is immigration. America must do something about immigration *now*.

On no issue have a Republican administration and Republicans in the House and Senate more blatantly or more cynically sold out conservatives and our country. Their inaction on this issue – or worse, proposals that would deepen the sea of immigrants, such as amnesty – are a scandal and a disgrace. Our forefathers, who were made of sterner stuff, would have met these legislators with torches and pitchforks, tar and feathers.

There are many reasons why we need to halt illegal immigration and further restrict legal immigration. Two are central to the next conservatism: national security and preserving traditional American culture.

The national security issue is clear. We are being invaded. In a world of Fourth Generation war, invasion by immigrants who do not assimilate is more dangerous than invasion by a foreign army. At some point, a foreign army will go home. But immigrants stay, and unassimilated immigrants provide an ongoing base for Fourth Generation war here in America. Our grandchildren may have to fight that war, and if they do, they will curse us for the folly of leaving our borders open.

The threat to our culture is no less serious. The cultural Marxists want open borders because one way to destroy our traditional American culture is to bury it under tens of millions of immigrants from alien cultures. Not only do the cultural Marxists welcome the immigrants, by demanding "multiculturalism" they ensure that these immigrants do not assimilate. Multiculturalism condemns any attempt to Americanize immigrants and encourages them to retain their own cultures, the defects of which caused them to leave their own countries in the first place.

Paul Weyrich's father was an immigrant. He came to America as a young man in the 1920s, from Germany. Like other immigrants in his time and before, he worked hard to become an American. The household Paul grew up in spoke English, not German. They lived just like other Americans who had been here for generations. Paul's father would have regarded multiculturalism as both stupid and dangerous. He would have been right on both counts.

The next conservatism needs to recognize that when it comes to immigration policy, neither the Democrats nor the Republicans are our friends. The Democrats want open borders because most of them are cultural Marxists. The Republicans agree because Wall Street wants cheap labor. The next conservatism is not in Wall Street's pocket. Our country is more important than Wall Street's profits.

Conservatives need to make it clear that we will not vote for any candidate who refuses to close our borders to illegal immigration and greatly reduce legal immigration, at least until we can Americanize the immigrants we already have. More, we will actively support candidates, including in primaries, who promise to do whatever is necessary to control our borders.

If we do not halt the flow of Third World immigrants into our country, all other aspects of national security will become irrelevant, because soon enough we will have no nation to secure.

Chapter Five

Governing America: Economic Security

Some readers may wonder at the title of this chapter. "Since when," they may think, "have conservatives believed that government ought to provide economic security?"

That is not quite what we are suggesting here. It is the left that believes government somehow "owes" economic security to everyone, however lazy their days or imprudent their habits. Nowadays, Republicans seem to go along, at least when it is a question of bailing out some Wall Street investment bank. The Washington Establishment is united on privatizing gains and socializing losses, for rich and poor alike.

The next conservatism should not agree. When government breaks the natural, age-old relationship between risk and reward – the higher the reward, the greater the risk; the safer the course, the less the gain – it undermines important virtues. Prudence, saving, abhorring debt, modest living, security gained by hard work and thrift, all go out the window. If carried far enough, privatizing profits and socializing losses makes risk and debt the only "sound" investments.

When we suggest that governing America includes economic security, we merely recognize that American governments at all levels, federal, state and local, from the founding of the republic onward have played roles in our economy.

The question is what those roles should be. The next conservatism, respecting the limits inherent in a restored republic, should seek, not a government that provides economic security, but one that creates conditions in which people can provide their own economic security.

Infrastructure

Libertarians may argue that government should play no economic role, but that is not the American tradition. From the beginning, government, including the federal government, acted to create conditions under which agriculture, commerce, and industry could flourish. One example, on which we have already touched, is providing infrastructure.

The first federally funded highway, the famed National Road that connected America's east and west across the Allegheny Mountains, was approved by Congress in the March 29, 1806 "Act to Regulate the Laying Out and Making a Road from Cumberland, in the State of Maryland, to the State of Ohio."

A study by Lawrence J. Malone, *Opening the West: Federal Internal Improvements Before 1860*, concludes that up to the Civil War states spent about $300 million on transportation infrastructure, local governments about $125 million, and the federal government about $54 million. In today's dollars, those would be many billions.

The technological shift from roads and canals to railroads saw substantial government involvement in creating a new rail infrastructure. Carter Goodrich, the dean of infrastructure studies, wrote in his seminal book, *Government Promotion of American Canals and Railroads 1800–1890*:

For eleven states of the South, it has been estimated

that public agencies contributed well over 55 percent of the cost of all railroad construction before 1861 and at least 75 percent of the amount made available in cash. Of the four trunk-line railroads that reached Lake Erie or the Ohio River by 1855, public sources had provided about half of the funds for the Pennsylvania, the Baltimore and Ohio, and the Erie. . . .

In the period after 1860, there is a marked change in the relative contributions of the different levels of government. The Era of National Subsidy, which was initiated with the Illinois Central [Railroad] Act of 1850, reached its peak in the few years following the end of the Civil War. The companies that constructed the first transcontinental railroad received [federal] loans of nearly $65,000,000. In addition, land grants were authorized during the years 1861–72 to a number of railroad companies, from which they ultimately obtained well over 100,000,000 acres.

The 20th century brought the rise of the automobile, and with it massive government subsidy of highway infrastructure. Fifty years ago, the federal government passed the National Defense Interstate Highway Act and began building the interstate highway system, at a cost that now exceeds $114 billion.

The next conservatism should accept this precedent. Its agenda should include providing adequate national and local infrastructure. Our economy cannot flourish without it. With the end of cheap oil, we need not merely to maintain and repair the existing highway-based transportation infrastructure, but to build once again a rail infrastructure adequate for both freight and passengers. Many of our cities need funds to maintain and upgrade another important type of infrastructure, water and sewer systems. Doing so is a legitimate function of government.

Currency

So is another of the federal government's most important duties, ensuring that our currency retains its value. Inflation is the cruelest tax, because it is a tax on savings. Inflation eats away at the value of savings like moths eat woolens.

Here, the federal government has failed us. The dollar has lost value over time to an alarming degree. As recently as the early 1970s, it was possible to buy a good new car for around $2,000. Now that figure is $20,000. The dollar has lost 90% of its value in less than four decades.

The next conservatism should make fighting inflation and guaranteeing the long-term value of the dollar one of its top economic goals. There are a number of ways this might be accomplished. One is returning to the gold standard. Another is to measure the value of a dollar by the price of a "market basket" of goods ordinary people buy. We might want to specify in law that the Federal Reserve Bank's most important responsibility is to prevent inflation. However we go about it, we should allow Americans to be confident that the dollar they save today will still be worth a dollar when they retire. Nothing is more important for the economic security of the middle class.

Economics

These two actions, providing the infrastructure trade and industry require and ensuring our currency retains its value, illustrate the next conservative economics. What do we see if we stand back a bit and look at economics as a whole?

The next conservatism's economics should start by

putting economics itself in its proper place. Today, most people seem to accept the primacy of the economy. Anything is good if it helps the economy, bad if it hurts the economy. That is not the traditional conservative view. We used to have higher standards.

Economics is utilitarian, and conservative thought has rightly rejected utilitarianism since the days of poor, unhinged Jeremy Bentham. In *The Conservative Mind*, Russell Kirk describes Marxism as Bentham's "Utilitarianism flavored with Hegel and converted to the uses of the revolutionary proletariat." As conservatives, we ought to reject Marxism *per et fils*.

Even less have conservatives made economic efficiency their idol. If economic efficiency means, for example, that America should send all its manufacturing jobs overseas, as free trade seems to demand, the next conservatism should not say, "Oh, well, I guess we have to go along with it." Better we toss our *sabots* into free trade's grinding gears. Economic security requires that people be able to get good-paying jobs, which means manufacturing jobs.

The next conservatism needs to start with what conservatives have gotten right about economics, then build on that base to address some problems we have largely ignored. Among the things conservatives have gotten right are the need for lower marginal income and capital gains tax rates (in terms of economic effects, how tax cuts are structured are as or more important than how deeply taxes are cut), the desirability of a flat tax and of replacing the income tax with some form of consumption tax (which requires a Constitutional amendment to once again make an income tax illegal, lest we end up with both an income and a consumption tax), and the importance of cutting federal spending. Here we see how one part of the next conservative agenda supports another: restoring the republic, adopting a foreign policy for Americans and military reform should together reduce the federal budget by hundreds of billions of dollars annually.

What are the new economic challenges the next conservatism must face in order to create the conditions for economic security? Here are some samples, all of them important, none of them easy:

* We must restore American manufacturing. Unless we are willing quietly to become a Third World country, we need to make things. We must stop the movement of our manufacturing to China and other foreign countries. We must conserve and restore the well-paying jobs manufacturing offers to the blue-collar middle class, a class whose existence ought to be one of our proudest national achievements.

* We need to restore thrift as a basis of our economy in place of consumption. A habit of thrift is essential for economic security. Part of the reason we are selling America off piece-by-piece to foreigners is that Americans save so little. Two-thirds of the American economy is now based on consumer spending, and much of the money spent on consumer goods is borrowed. That is not sustainable, and it points toward a crash. The next conservative economics needs to reward thrift, which adopting a consumption tax in place of the income tax would accomplish. Thrift allows citizens to provide their own economic security instead of depending on the "nanny state" to bail them out.

* The next conservatism favors free enterprise. But is enterprise truly free if there are no limits on its scale? Big business is outsourcing jobs overseas as fast as it can. Would small businesses that are anchored in their

communities do that? Probably not. Are local entrepreneurs free if they have to compete against huge chains of big-box stores that sell almost nothing made in America? They are free only to go out of business. The next conservatism should define free enterprise more broadly, looking not just at the danger from government but also at the threat to average Americans' economic security from vast corporations, many of them multi-nationals that could care less about America's future. Traditionally, conservatives have favored things that are local and small-scale: Think locally, act locally. Giving people the ability to act locally would seem to require cutting huge corporations down to size.

Each of these issues illustrates the requirement to put economics itself, and especially that hobgoblin of Globalists and utilitarians, economic efficiency, back in its place. The Dow Jones is not the measure of all things, nor ought life be just about getting and spending. Creating the conditions for economic security reaches beyond economics.

Energy Policy

One area into which it reaches forcefully is energy policy. When gas cost up to $4 per gallon, no one who drove a car needed to be told that we have an energy crisis on our hands. The immediate crisis may past. But 2008's spike in oil and gasoline prices is a harbinger of things to come.

The fact is, we may be facing "peak oil."[1] In the 1950s, American Shell Oil scientist M. King Hubbert identified

---

1   The following discussion is drawn from an essay written for Free Congress Foundation by Rep. Roscoe G. Bartlett of Maryland.

"peak oil." He discovered that oil field production follows a bell curve that rises to a maximum, or peak, when about half the oil is extracted. After that peak, production declines. The U.S. hit "peak oil" in 1971, and American oil production has declined every year since. The U.S. has only 3 percent of world oil reserves. We contribute eight percent of world production. We are pumping our precious reserves rapidly, following a policy that might be called "drain America first." Future generations may curse us for leaving America with no oil of its own. Meanwhile, from importing one-third of the oil we used before the Arab oil embargo of 1973, we now import about two-thirds. To put it bluntly, we are drunk on oil.

Hubbert was right about the U.S. What about the world? Oil production is declining in 33 of the world's largest oil-producing countries. Experts agree global peak oil is inevitable. Many predict it is imminent. Neither high oil prices nor technological advances have reversed production declines after the peak. Despite periods of high prices and new technologies, world oil discoveries have steadily declined for 40 years.

What does the prospect of global peak oil mean for the next conservatism? Prudence forbids conservatives to bet on the outcome, expecting that new technologies will somehow enable us to go on living the way we have, wasting vast amounts of energy. That may happen, but we cannot count on it. If our goal is economic security, our agenda must be based on more than hope. As the old saying goes, hope makes a good breakfast but a poor dinner.

The proposed National Defense Public Transportation Act would be a step in the right direction. By creating a new infrastructure of bus routes, streetcar lines, electric interurban railways and electrified main line railroads, the Act would help free America from dependence on imported oil.

But conservatives know that big problems can seldom if ever be solved by government programs alone. In the long run, like everything else, economic security depends upon private virtue. In this case, virtue means conservation. We all need to use less energy, which requires using energy wisely. Conservatives should set the example, walking or cycling for local errands (40% of all automobile trips are to destinations less than two miles away), taking public transportation to work, insulating our homes and opening the windows on nice days instead of running the air conditioning. Again we see the virtue in Retroculture; this is how our grandparents lived.

Business

Creating the conditions for economic security means helping business to flourish. That sounds like standard conservative thinking. But the next conservatism is rightly suspicious of big corporations. Like big government, big businesses care little if at all what effects their actions have locally. Conservatives or not, "locally" is where we all live.

Small businesses usually do care about the local effects of their actions. Their owners, managers, employees and customers often live in the local community. If they injure that community, small businesses hurt themselves.

Small businesses are also an important part of something America still does relatively well, namely creating economic opportunity and new jobs. A major reason we do that better than most of the world, including Europe, is that small businesses, especially new start-ups, face fewer government obstacles. In much of the world, someone who wants to start a new business faces a huge, hostile government bureaucracy. It can take him months or years (and often bribes) to get the many permissions and licenses he needs.

The next conservatism should build on America's success. Rather than resting happy in our superiority to other countries, we should make establishing a new business even easier.

At present, while starting a new business is less difficult than in most places, it can still be daunting. Immediately, the person who wants to set up shop faces an array of federal, state and local rules and regulations. He is deluged with pieces of government paper, many of which begin, "Under penalty of law . . ." The endless forms he must fill out are obscure and confusing. If he makes an honest mistake, he may be legally liable.

The next conservatism should seek to reduce this burden. Some of the rules, regulations and agencies should simply be abolished. Others, such as public health requirements for restaurants, are necessary. But where government imposes a requirement, it should also help people meet that requirement.

Whenever government lays a reporting or other regulatory requirement on small businesses, it should offer a bureau to which a business can turn, without charge or fee, for help in meeting the requirement. The bureau would provide advice on how to meet the substance of the requirement and help fill out the government paperwork. In effect, this bureau would be a type of ombudsman. An ombudsman is a government employee whose job is to help ordinary citizens deal with other government offices.

Ombudsman

Here is an example of what we mean. Let us say someone is good at repairing small appliances (as conservatives, we would rather repair something old than buy something new). He decides to set up a small business to offer appliance repairs. Immediately, he faces multiple government requirements, each with a large amount of paperwork and complex forms. Now, he is very good at repairing appliances, but he knows nothing about legal forms. Most of them seem incomprehensible to him.

Instead of having to hire a lawyer with money he probably does not have, he can turn to his local small business ombudsman. The ombudsman not only walks him through what the requirements mean and offers suggestions of how to meet them, he sits down with him and helps him fill out the forms. If there is a mistake, other government offices return the form to the ombudsman for correction rather than taking legal action against the new business. The ombudsman's job is to get the business up and going by running interference for the small business owner, and he has the legal authority to do that.

This is one way the next conservatism could be helpful to inner-city residents, minorities and immigrants. Many of these people have skills that could be the basis of a small business. But they have no idea how to deal with government, and they are often afraid of the government. Right in their neighborhood would be a small business ombudsman's office they could go to for all the help and assurance they would need. The burdens imposed by government would fall at least partly on government, instead of serving as a crippling tax on enterprise.

Good New Taxes

Some conservatives believe all taxes are bad. The next conservatism should not agree. There is an old saying that, "If you want less of something, tax it." That is the rationale for "sin taxes," high taxes on substances such as cigarettes and alcohol.

One thing the next conservatism should want less of is outsourcing American jobs overseas. Outsourcing has been one of the unfortunate consequences of free trade. Free trade says, "Unless you will work for less money, we will just move your job overseas."

This is a case where the Democrats are betraying their base, just as the Republican party has betrayed its conservative base on issues such as immigration and government spending. American workers, especially those in manufacturing, have traditionally voted Democratic. When Democrats support free trade and unlimited outsourcing of American jobs overseas, they are giving American workers a kick in the pants. Why do many Democratic Senators and Congressmen support free trade? The answer, as usual in Washington, is "follow the money." The interests that benefit from free trade give millions of dollars to politicians of both parties.

If we want to stop or at least reduce the outsourcing of American jobs overseas, we should tax outsourcing. The next conservatism should see that as a good new tax. One way to do it might be to levy export duties on outsourcing.

When we think of duties and tariffs, we usually think of tariffs on imports. But for centuries, many countries also had export duties on some products. What if we put an export duty of, say, 500% on every job companies here send overseas? The company would have to pay an annual tax of five times the wage of the new employee it hired or contracted overseas. Businesses might find it made better economic sense to keep that job in America.

The next conservatism should reconsider the conventional wisdom about tariffs generally. Virtually the whole Washington Establishment now sings the song, "All tariffs are bad; free trade is good." But America became a powerful manufacturing nation under tariff protection. Is the past perhaps trying to tell us something?

As we have already noted, America cannot have

economic security unless it makes things. An economy built on financial manipulation, which is what we have now, is highly insecure. A financial panic, where credit dries up, can bring the whole pyramid down. Nor can a "service economy" offer average people an opportunity for economic security. Most service jobs do not pay enough to raise a family on. Both parents have to work, and even then they often cannot pay the bills.

Good-paying jobs are mostly manufacturing jobs. If the next conservatism is serious about creating the conditions for economic security, it needs to make the restoration of American manufacturing one of its top priorities. If that requires tariffs, so be it. The next conservatism should be about serving Main Street, not Wall Street.

Pro-Labor Conservatism

From this perspective, the next conservatism is pro-labor. That is not the same thing as being pro-union. Over the past half-century, labor union presence in American life has declined greatly. In the 1940s, a single union, John L. Lewis's United Mine Workers, could and did hold the whole country hostage. Today, only about 12% of American workers are union members.

Most conservatives see this as a good thing, and in some ways it is. But the next conservatism should be for, not against, American workers. Most of the people who work in manufacturing are cultural conservatives. We should stand up for these people and what they need for economic security, a job that pays a family wage. A family wage is a wage that pays a head of household enough to give his family a middle-class standard of living with his wife staying home to take care of their children.

That means conservatives should be willing to work with some unions, unions that actually stand for their members' economic interests. The leadership of most of the big unions could care less about the well-being of their members. They use their compulsory dues to support all kinds of culturally Marxist "causes" that most of their members rightly despise. At the same time, they go along with their buddies in the Washington Establishment on issues such as free trade, thereby selling their union's members out. They are completely out of touch with their base.

This gives the next conservatism a political opportunity. While we should work with smaller unions that are in touch with their members and really represent them, the next conservatism should include a plan for "trust-busting" the big unions that sell their members out. Specifics of such a plan could include:

* Enforcing regulations already on the books to require more transparency in union expenditure. If the big unions' members could see the kind of culturally Marxist causes to which their dues go, they would demand changes or form new unions.
* Inform union members of the Beck decision, which ruled that workers were not obligated to pay union dues that are used for causes unrelated to workers' interests.
* Eliminate all requirements for compulsory unionism, so unions would have to compete for members by actually representing their interests.

The next conservatism should also distinguish between unions in private industries and those that represent public sector workers. Not only are many of the latter's leaders deeply into cultural Marxism, so in some cases are many of their members. Conservatives should bring these unions' legitimacy into question. Public employees can have no legitimate right to strike, because their wages are paid by citizens' taxes. If they strike, they are biting the hand that feeds them.

In sum, the next conservatism should see labor and unions as differentiated rather than as all the same. Labor, in the form of smaller unions that represent their members' genuine economic interests such as the provision of good-paying manufacturing jobs, is not our opponent. It can be our partner in creating conditions in which people can find economic security. The "fat cat" leaders of the big unions, detached as they are from their members' interests and devoted to radical politics, should be a target for conservatives and union members alike. In unions as in business and in agriculture, the next conservatism should favor small scale, because small scale means local control and local control gives ordinary people a voice.

Tort Reform

Our final example of the next conservative economics illustrates the connection between the "dismal science" and culture: tort reform. No, this has not suddenly become a cookbook; the word for the wonderful Austrian cakes is torte, not tort. As even a wise lawyer will allow, tortes are much to be preferred over torts (our favorite is *Malakofftorte*), but it is torts that need reforming. *Black's Law Dictionary* defines a tort as "A civil wrong for which remedy may be obtained, usually in the form of damages." In simpler terms, if somebody harms somebody else or their property, and does so negligently, he has committed a tort. It is not necessary that he has broken a law.

Lawsuits are about torts, and America is drowning in lawsuits. Many are phony, mere schemes to bilk someone of their money. Often, they are driven by shyster lawyers who are paid on contingency, i.e., they get a percentage of the take if they win. Put bluntly, it is a racket.

Vice President Dan Quayle's single, fleeting moment of popularity came when, in a speech on something else, he happened to call for tort reform. He never did it again. Why not? The fact that the Trial Lawyers Association is the single largest donor of money to both political parties may have had something to do with it.

The next conservatism should make tort reform a plank in its platform, the trial lawyers be hanged. The economic cost is in the hundreds of billions of dollars annually, money we all pay in the form of higher insurance premiums, huge medical bills, and more costly goods and services.

The cultural damage is worse. A republic requires citizens who take responsibility for their actions. Out-of-control lawsuits, in contrast, feed a "victim" mindset, which is just what cultural Marxism wants. Somebody smokes himself into cancer; it's the tobacco companies' fault. A baby is born defective; it's the obstetrician's fault (malpractice insurance is one of the main reasons for high medical costs). Someone eats himself into a place on walrus beach; it's the restaurants' fault. Lawsuits fly, and because it is often less expensive to the insurance company to settle than to fight the case, the scam is rewarded. Being a "victim" pays.

The "victim" mindset undermines our culture in two ways. First, it feeds the desire for a nanny state. Second, it makes people and companies afraid to take any risk lest they get sued. Don't let the neighborhood kids play in your yard; if one of them gets hurt, you might get sued. Wait for the police or other emergency personnel in a crisis; if you try to help someone, they might sue you (so you let them drown instead). When the authors of this book were boys, they were often invited up into the cabs of locomotives by the engineers, who were friendly to kids who liked trains. Not anymore; they and the railroad might face a lawsuit. As conservatives' old friend Scrooge would say, "Bah! Humbug!" Humbuggery it is, too, most of it anyway. The next conservatism should put a stop to it.

One action that would at least diminish the lawsuit plague would be to outlaw contingency fees. They are illegal in most if not all European countries. A lawyer could only charge a set fee, and he would have to be paid whether his client won or lost. Fewer lawyers would chase ambulances if they did not see dollar signs flapping from them, and fewer "victims" of their own mistakes would sue if they had to pay their lawyer, win or lose. It might also make sense to compel the suer to pay the defendant's legal expenses as well as his own if he lost.

Another reform would be to limit the plaintiff's attorney's ability to challenge jurors. At present, many contingency-fee lawyers are masters at keeping anyone with a grain of common sense off the jury, through a question-and-answer process called *voir dire*. They want, and get, a jury of sympathetic saps who will fall for any sob story and look on a big award as a chance for someone like them to win the lottery. A true jury of "peers," not vetted by a shyster, will usually include a few folks who can tell Shinola from that other stuff. A few is usually enough to get a verdict in line with the facts.

The trial lawyers will go to any lengths to prevent tort reform, because it threatens to tear a hole in their feed bags. Their money will pile up on politicians' desks like lawyers stacked up in Hell. But this is an issue the next conservatism can win. Millions of Americans who do not think of themselves as conservatives would join in this cause. Who isn't tired of looking over his shoulder all the time, wondering if he is going to get sued?

Tort reform returns us to where we started: the next

conservative economics is about more than economics. If we want to create conditions in which people can build their own economic security, we must look beyond tax rates, Federal Reserve Bank policy, even balanced budgets. Those things remain important, but they are not sufficient. Culture, morals, the nature of citizenship in a free republic, even what it means to be a country are all part of conservative economic governance. All of these set the conditions under which economic security is possible – or not. Increasingly, for middle class Americans, economic security is a vanishing dream. The next conservative economics can turn that around, because conservatives understand that private virtue is the most important public good.

Chapter Six

Governing America: Moral Security

For almost half a century, America's traditional culture and those of us who try to live by its rules have been under assault. We are mocked, sneered at, called ignorant and "prejudiced." The values we hold, which are best summarized in the Ten Commandments, are denounced as "oppressive." Behavior we regard as wrong and sinful is flung in our faces, and if we dare object, we are damned as "intolerant," "insensitive" and "bigoted." It is all enough to give bigotry a good name.

The times are evil. We live in an age of moral and intellectual confusion, where down is called up and we are told we must see black as white. Russell Kirk quotes from a letter John Adams wrote in 1805, which perhaps better describes our day than his:

> I am willing you should call this the Age of Frivolity, as you do: and should not object if you had named it the Age of Folly, Vice, Frenzy, Fury, Brutality, Daemons . . . or the Age of the burning Brand from the bottomless Pit; or anything else but the Age of Reason.

Today, those who manufacture the popular culture abhor morals and reason alike. The most important question in the universe, so they tell us, is, "How do you feel right now about yourself?"

Like all great historical currents, the moral decay of Western societies has many causes. "Luxury" is one, against which the Founding Father warned us. Democracy, carried to an extreme where "what everyone does" must be right, is another. Dr. Kirk quotes Federalist Fisher Ames of Dedham, Massachusetts: "A democratick society will soon find its morals the incumbrance of its race, the surly companion of its licentious joys . . ." The most powerful cause of the West's moral dissolution is its loss of faith in the Christian religion. Culture, as Kirk said, comes from the cult.

All these things contribute to a falling away from traditional morality. But the vicious assault on age-old morals we witness and suffer from now can be traced directly to cultural Marxism. One of the Frankfurt School's proudest products was "Critical Theory." Critical Theory seeks to attain what Nietzsche called "the transvaluation of all values" – the old sins become virtues, and the old virtues become sins – by unremittingly, viciously criticizing every traditional belief and institution. Monogamy, the family (both labeled "patriarchy"), the church, traditional school curricula, white people (all "racists"), heterosexuals ("breeders"), men ("sexists"), anything and everything that derives from or upholds traditional society and culture are to be rendered odious by endless criticism. The message is not confined to academic environments; through television and other mass media, the public is psychologically conditioned to see all things past as "evil." Anyone who demurs is supposed to look in the mirror and see "another Hitler."

A Space for Moral Security

The next conservatism must offer a defense against this

assault. It is too much to call for returning society to its old moral foundations. God may accomplish that, or events, but at present it is beyond conservatives' powers.

Rather, the next conservatism must seek to create a space where those of us who live according to the old rules can do so safely. This is what we mean by "moral security." Moral security is the recognition of our right to live and believe as we wish, without facing constant assault.

Conservatives should be clear that moral security is defensive. It is not a call to use the power of the state to re-impose traditional morals on an unwilling society. That would contradict the next conservatism's call to restore the republic. Nor could such an attempt succeed, because culture is more powerful than politics.

Moral security does rightly demand that the state back away from its efforts to impose cultural Marxism on us. There is a clear and present danger that, under the rubric of "hate crimes," government may soon make expression of many of our beliefs illegal. As just one example, the left would dearly love to make any condemnation of homosexuality unlawful, as "hate." It has already become so on many university campuses. There, students who dare oppose homosexual activism face disciplinary proceedings and "sensitivity training," which is psychological conditioning to accept cultural Marxism's commands.

But most of the assault on traditional culture and morals does not stem from government. Rather, it flows in a Niagara-like torrent from the popular culture: from television, movies, music (especially music targeted at young people), advertisements, video games, newspapers, magazines – the list is endless. Of course, the public schools also play an important role in this assault. Sooner or later, we will see an attempt to forbid home schooling, through which more than a million children have escaped at least one conditioning mechanism.

Cultural conservatives will agree, we think, on the need for moral security. Like other minorities, we have a right to protection from a tyrannical majority. That has always been a principle of republican government.

The question is one of means. How can we create a safe "space" for traditional morals and the people who live by them? Here, the next conservatism has something new to suggest. It is drawn not from religion, nor from philosophy, nor from politics, but from the New Urbanism. What is it? A moral transect.

New Urbanism's "Smart Code"

It may be useful to review what the New Urbanism means by the transect. The transect is the basis of New Urbanism's "Smart Code." The "Smart Code" says you may build whatever you want, but not always where you want. The transect divides the land into six naturally-occurring zones:

* T-1: Natural, i.e. unbuilt land.
* T-2: Rural, mostly farms.
* T-3: Suburban
* T-4: General urban, i.e. "streetcar suburbs."
* T-5: Urban center.
* T-6: Urban core.

Certain types of structures, densities, streets, and activities are appropriate to the nature of each zone in the transect. Building something inappropriate to the zone, literally "out of place" in that zone, is not permitted. However, unless it is intended to house an illegal activity, it can almost certainly be built somewhere else, in a different zone.

It is important to note that the transect is both *descriptive* and *prescriptive*. The six zones are not arbitrary. They occur naturally. They are observable throughout much of the world and most of human history. The transect is describing a traditional pattern which has worked over time.

But the transect is simultaneously *prescriptive*. It sets down rules that must be followed. Those rules are based on tradition, but the Smart Code makes them more than traditions. A code is a rule. Why is it necessary to move beyond traditions to rules? Because the New Urbanism recognizes that since World War II, America has abandoned age-old traditions, with disastrous results. Sometimes traditions can only be recovered by laying down rules.

The Moral Transect

The moral transect would work similarly. It would allow any legal activity, however repugnant to cultural conservatives, in its appropriate place. But it could not be done everywhere. Where would such activities be disallowed? Wherever they would force themselves on Americans whose traditional, Judeo-Christian morals condemn them.

Sex education in the public schools offers an example. Millions of Americans who try to live by traditional moral rules have no alternative but to send their children to the public schools. Both parents have to work, so they cannot homeschool. Nor can they afford to send their children to private schools. Unfortunately, most public schools teach "sex education" that contradicts traditional morals. It accepts that children will be having sex long before they marry. Often, it promotes homosexuality. The moral transect would say that public schools are not appropriate places to teach such material. Doing so is a direct assault on both children and parents who reject the new "anything goes" sexual morality and strive to uphold traditional sexual morals.

Similarly, violent material or material that portrays sex should not be allowed on broadcast television before the hour when good children are in bed, say nine o'clock. The rule would apply not only to programming but also to advertisements and promotions. Cable and satellite television providers would be given a choice: they could either abide by the transect's rule or they could allow their customers to receive (and pay for) only those channels they want, instead of having to buy a "package" that includes trash such as MTV. The transect would allow television networks to put on whatever they wanted to, but not always when they wanted to.

Developing the New Urbanist transect took years of work and the efforts of many people. The moral transect will require as much or more. In fact, the moral transect is more complex, because it applies to time as well as place, and to almost every aspect of our culture. We can only offer the idea of a moral transect here, not the transect itself. We encourage other cultural conservatives to devote both time and thought to its construction.

Like the New Urbanist transect, the moral transect must be both descriptive and prescriptive. It should not be arbitrary. Rather, it should reflect what occurred naturally through most of American history. Immoral activities are not new. But past generations understood that they had their places and times, and were not to be seen outside those places and times. Cities had their "adult bookstores," but they were confined to the tenderloin district or "Hell's corner." (Mr. Lind recalls a young Quaker telling him, "I was so excited when I first saw a sign for an 'Adult Bookstore.' I thought, "Oh, wonderful! They'll have Spinoza!'")

The moral transect will offer cultural conservatives the moral security that is their right, security from having immorality thrust upon them. But it is not censorship, because everything currently legal is still permitted. All that is regulated is where, when and to whom sin can be purveyed as an attractive commodity. History assures us that those who want it will find it. The rest of us will no longer have to fear emerging from church to find a "Gay Pride" parade going by (the homosexuals will still be allowed their "Gay Pride" parade, which neatly combines two sins, but not on Sunday and in their own part of town).

The question arises as to who will lay down and enforce the codes derived from the moral transect. For the New Urbanist transect, the answer is usually local governments. The same will often be true for the moral transect. At times, state governments might become involved. Both allow for local and regional variation, which conservatives have traditionally approved. We do not expect San Francisco to be Cleveland, just as the gays should not expect Cleveland to become San Francisco. Federal government intervention should occur rarely if at all; its instruments are mostly too heavy and too blunt.

But for the most part, the next conservatism should envision codes derived from the moral transect being enforced through the marketplace. The primary source of cultural and moral degradation is the popular culture, and it is a commercialized culture. While cultural conservatives are probably now a minority, we are a sizable minority. We can move the commercializers of popular culture toward acceptance of the moral transect, and our right to moral security, through the power of the purse. For example, if millions of moral traditionalists cut off their cable or satellite television service until they were allowed to buy only the networks they wanted, or the companies agreed to the "nine o'clock" rule, they would almost certainly prevail.

Operating through the marketplace and the power of

the purse, however, demands of conservatives a new level of organization, and also a somewhat different orientation. At present, not only is the conservative movement fragmented, dispirited and largely leaderless, it is also focused almost entirely on politics. As we have already emphasized, politics must remain important to conservatives. But if the next conservatism is to create moral security, promote Retroculture or achieve its other goals, it must extend beyond politics. We need a new conservative movement that is also a different kind of movement, one that reflects the fact that conservatism is not an ideology but a way of life.

Chapter Seven

The Next Conservative Movement

One of the casualties of the Bush administration was the conservative movement. By labeling "conservative" policies that were starkly anti-conservative, such as Wilsonianism in foreign affairs, open borders and Globalism, the Bush White House disillusioned and disappointed the conservative grass roots. Many activists gave up and went home. At the same time, Republican favors and money suborned the movement's Washington leadership, turning most of it into a claque for the White House. Some conservative leaders outside Washington were also sucked in, although leaders of the Religious Right generally remained true to their calling. In reality, the conservative movement must now be spoken of in the past tense. It no longer exists.

The Bush administration is not entirely to blame. Both of the authors of this book have been involved in the conservative movement since they were in high school, back in the Pleistocene. Paul Weyrich can honestly claim to have been one of the movement's godfathers. In some ways the conservative movement achieved more than its founders ever dreamed it could, back in the 1960s and 1970s. Then, most people thought of conservatism as a marginal force that had been killed and buried with Barry Goldwater's defeat in 1964. The idea that conservatism could in just a few decades come to represent the American mainstream while liberalism was politically marginalized would have been unimaginable. Yet that was the very real achievement of the old conservative movement.

But in that success lay the seeds of the movement's destruction. In its early stages, as an outsider, every political movement can be true to its agenda. But once it takes power, it inevitably comes to find much of its agenda politically inconvenient. The agenda gets in the way of making deals, gaining more power and collecting money. In time, it ceases to be a real movement and joins the Establishment. The Bush administration accelerated this process by cynically misusing the term "conservative," but the dynamic is inherent in all movements.

This is why the next conservatism requires a new conservative movement. Let there be no doubt that without the backing of a grass roots movement, the next conservatism is but straws in the wind. Ideas on paper do not alone restore a sinking nation. They must be translated into action, which requires either a grass roots movement or a coup. As conservatives, we are not much in favor of coups.

Were it still alive, the old conservative movement would not meet today's needs. The old movement, with a few exceptions such as the homeschoolers, was just about politics. As we have said repeatedly, the next conservatism needs to be about more than politics. Politics remains important. It is the only means for restoring the republic. But we cannot win the culture war through politics.

The next conservatism needs not only a new movement, it needs a new kind of movement, a movement of people dedicated to restoring the old ways of living in their own lives and the lives of their families. The next conservative movement is perhaps best imagined as a community of men and women devoted to the old virtues of modest living, hard work, self-sufficiency, prudence (which includes not running after every new thing), thrift, conservation, and living God-centered rather than world-centered lives. If we want to restore our old culture, we must begin by living according to the old culture's rules.

Once we acknowledge the need for a new conservative movement that is also a new kind of movement, the question becomes, how do we build such a movement?

We start with what is already happening. Here, there is a good deal of encouraging news. If we look around the country, we see a growing number of Americans withdrawing from the materialist, commercialized, sexualized, culturally Marxist popular culture and taking their lives and the lives of their families in different directions. Not all these different directions fit within the next conservatism, but surprisingly many do.

The most obvious example, and a highly important component of the next conservative movement, is the homeschoolers. Most homeschooled children are receiving a traditional education. They are studying the history and reading the literature of Western, Judeo-Christian civilization. They are learning how to do arithmetic without calculators and how to write and speak with correct grammar. They have increasing opportunities to go on after their homeschooling to colleges and universities that offer genuine education instead of Political Correctness. All this is an enormous achievement, and it points to what the next conservative movement should look like. It is an action that changes the way people live.

Conservatives are comfortable with homeschooling because it is something we initiated. There are other movements conservatives did not initiate that also fit within the next conservatism. One is the movement to "kill your television," especially in homes with children. We have all seen the contrast between active, imaginative children who are reared in homes without television (and video games) and the sad, brain-dead blobs who have been plopped in front of the box almost from birth (television now offers programming for two-year olds, on PBS no less). Television is the Devil's baby-sitter. It is an easy way to keep kids quiet and "entertained" ("entertainment" has become America's favorite drug), but it does children vast long-term damage. "Kill your television" did not start as a conservative slogan, but it integrates quite nicely into the next conservatism.

So does the movement to live sustainably, what the next conservatism calls living intensive instead of extensive lives. The intensive life uses fewer things and resources but uses them more thoughtfully and gets more out of them. Examples of the intensive or sustainable life range from having a family vegetable garden, hanging out the wash instead of using a dryer, cycling or walking to run errands and taking the train instead of the car to work through establishing an organic family farm that sells its products locally. All these actions and many more like them are con- servative because they represent a return to the way Americans used to live. They are Retroculture in action.

The next conservative movement should build bridges among these and other people who, for a variety of reasons and from a variety of political backgrounds, are resurrect- ing the old ways in their own lives. The popular culture tells anyone who tries to reject it, "You are all alone. You cannot possibly succeed. There is something wrong with you." It is hard for isolated individuals to stand against these assaults. But if individuals are tied in with other peo- ple who reject popular culture, resistance becomes easier. There really is strength in numbers.

This can be how the next conservative movement begins. But if it is to grow, it must follow some rules that apply to all political movements. Paul Weyrich was recognized as one of the "master mechanics" of movement building, and he saw few movements succeed without following these rules.

The first step is to identify a target list. Who do you want to reach? For the most part, your target list will be people and organizations that already share some of your views. Those are the people who are most likely to be interested in what your new movement wants to accomplish.

Next, you need to send out field teams to do audits. You want to audit each potential ally on its own ground. Your audit asks questions such as:

* What local organizations are effective?
* What is their home ground?
* Whom do they reach?
* How do they communicate?
* Who are their most effective leaders?

Your audit is your map. It tells you the lay of the land, so you know who to talk to, who is real and who is not.

Then, you need to identify your leader or champion. He has to be someone other people can look to as a leader, and he has to be someone who is willing to take risks. You cannot build a new movement by playing it safe all the time. As Napoleon said, if you want to make an omelet, you have to break some eggs.

For the next conservative movement, selecting a leader will be a critical challenge. The leader needs great strength of character, and there are not many people like that on the political horizon. Lots of phonies will come forward, hoping a leadership role will enable them to gain power and money for themselves. Most will try to short-circuit the new movement by leading it back into the Zombie embrace of the Republican Party. Beware!

Once a leader is chosen, the next step is to get your leader together with the people and organizations your audit had identified as potential allies. He needs a written statement of your new movement's goals. For the most part, anyone who will sign on to these goals can be part of your movement. There will be cases, however, where your leader has to recognize that some groups may be unacceptable to other groups your movement needs more.

Then comes the single most important element. As your coalition of interested groups and individuals grows, you must maintain constant communication with them. They must always be receiving something new and interesting from you, including not only information but also activities in which they can join. Constant communication is the lifeblood of any movement, and if it is not maintained, the movement will die. The internet and other technologies have made it much easier and less expensive to maintain constant communication than it used to be. Remember, however, that the next conservative movement will include some people who limit technology's presence in their lives and homes. You will need a low-tech means of communicating with them.

While your new movement's leadership must always be open to communications from your troops in the field, it is a mistake to think any movement will just "happen," bottom-up. For the most part, your troops will be asking you, "What should we do?" Your leadership must be pro-active in coming up with things for them to do, activities that will hold their interest while advancing your movement's goals.

This is a simplified version of the mechanics of movement-building, but it touches on all the basics. Remember, no matter how compelling your message, without the right mechanics it will go nowhere.

With a correct, proven approach to political mechanics,

there is no question a new movement can be built on the basis of the next conservatism. More and more Americans from all (or no) political backgrounds recognize that our country is going down the wrong road. When you have taken a wrong road, you have to turn back. People are ready for Retroculture.

Even though the mechanics will be similar, the next conservative movement will differ from the old conservative movement and from other political movements. Why? Because the next conservatism has a different view of power. In J.R.R. Tolkien's *Lord of the Rings*, which is one of the great Christian books of the 20th century, the ring of power represents power itself. Tolkien warns that in the long run it cannot be used for good, because ultimately it distorts whoever uses it to the point where they become evil. Regardless of their original intention, they end up wanting power over everyone else.

These warnings are consistent with what American conservatives have always believed. America's Founding Fathers devised a government of three competing branches to keep the federal government's power in check. Conservatives have also sought to keep government small, and to restrict its power through traditions, precedents and rights hallowed by time. Wise conservatives have realized that their task is not merely to put the right people in power, but to keep too much power out of anybody's hands, even the right people's.

Politics, of course, is about acquiring and using power. But the next conservatism will use power defensively, not offensively. We have made this point throughout this book, but we make it again here because it must become central to the work of the next conservative movement. We should not seek to use political power to ram our agenda down anyone else's throat. Rather, we should employ it to prevent government from ramming ideologies, social engineering, utopian schemes and other radical "improvements" down our throats.

The next conservative movement's offense should be rooted, not in political power, but in the power of example. It should seek to restore America from the bottom up, not the top down. Real restoration will come as free individuals decide to change the way they live their lives. This is what the Christian call to repent means. Forced repentance is a contradiction in terms, because it is not genuine. Repentance can only come from a change of mind and heart, which is best inspired by the power of example. It was thus that the Christian church grew from a tiny sect to the faith of much of the world.

Dependence on the power of example, the example of lives lived well in accordance with the Ten Commandments and the traditions of Western culture, places a heavy burden on the next conservative movement. It is much harder than merely winning elections. But unlike politics alone, it can win the war for Western culture.

Reliance on the power of example will protect the next conservative movement from abandoning its agenda as it grows strong. Abandoning its agenda would cost the next conservatism the power of example, weakening rather than strengthening the movement. Power and truth can remain united, unlike in purely political movements where truth at some point becomes an impediment to power and is discarded.

So the next conservative movement is just this: a growing coalition of people who are committed to living differently. They share a common rejection of the popular culture, of a life based on wants and instant gratification and subjugated to the dictates of cultural Marxism. They spurn and live apart from Brave New World. They seek to work with other Americans, and perhaps Europeans as well, who know the past was better than the present and seek to live as their forefathers did, by the rules of Western culture. They carry their quest into the political arena, but they use the power of the state only defensively. They look beyond politics to lives well lived in the old ways, as lamps for their neighbors footsteps, harbingers of a world restored and as testimonies to the only safe form of power, the power of example. We might add, as gifts to God as well.

Index